Wimarshaná was cast out from the country in which he grew up in 1992, and soon found himself marooned on one of its former tropical colonies. There he encountered a different and strange world—a world he was supposed to call home.

This is his last known work.

By WIMARSHANÁ

Citizens' Guide to the Third World

Post Politica

Colombo: A Critical Introspection

MODERN *Heresy*

wimarshaná

MODERN HERESY

Published by Squircle Subversive, New York

Cover illustration by Sahib Brown

ISBN: 978-0-9925837-6-7

Heresies

When I starved you fed,
When I teared you bled,
Dormant, in doubt,
When inspiration ran unto drought,
You were replenishing rain on parched phrase,
This sapling's leaves in praise,
Dreamt toward your smiling sunshine rays.

For Sabiha Onais

Countrydictory

Pursuit of happiness, life and liberty,
Founding Fathers enriched by slavery,

'Land of the Free' but 'Manifest Destiny',
For Red Indians cruel irony,

Reincarnation of democracy,
'*All men are created equal...*' but three-fifths if smuggled on a ship across the sea,
Took nearly two hundred years to legally redress the hypocrisy,

Pilgrim Fathers fleeing religious tyranny,
Separation of church and state but for many a country founded on Christianity,

The Union versus the Confederacy,
Emancipation or states' rights—even what they were fighting for we can't agree,

Reconstruction stymied by Jim Crow predictably,
Segregation: 'Separate but Equal'—naked lie plain to see,

'*Give me your huddled masses...*'—the land of opportunity,
A nation of immigrants undeniably,
Each wave attempting to 'build walls' behind them callously,

Vacillating between isolationism and fighting others' wars globally,
Post WWII making European powers give up their empires self-righteously,
But then machinating to breed banana republics imperially,

The Roaring Twenties and Prohibition simultaneously,
Flappers celebrating their new found independence to negro jazz defiantly,
Their still disenfranchised black sisters left to struggle on womanfully,

Its creed capitalism unabashedly,
Touting laissez-faire, invisible hand, small government dogmatically,
But from the Great Depression to the Great Recession running helplessly,
To Uncle Sam to bail free markets out paternally,
To save capitalism with New Deal to stimulus package clemency,

The brains behind the post-war consumerist boom fueled by technology,
Scientists from the enemy—Nazi Germany,

The Red Scare trumped up by Hoover and McCarthy,
The House Un-American Activities Committee,
On a witch-hunt which would make the Soviets brim with jealousy,

Sequestered by Redlining, GI Bill denying perfidy,
The 50s idyllic suburban white conservative orthodoxy,
Imploded by drugs, sex and rock-and-roll 60s counter-culture non-conformity,

Oh but a flash '*Tune in, turn on and drop out*', the spirit of Haight-Ashbury,
'Flower Power' and mind-opening LSD,
How short the trip from hippie to yuppie,

'*Ballots rightful successor to bullets*' believed Lincoln, but perversely,
From Honest Abe to Malcom X, MLK, Jack and Bobby Kennedy,
Political assassinations occur recurrently,
In a country that spends on law enforcement exorbitantly,

The Moon Landing—greatest pioneering giant leap of humanity,
Performed for Space Race vanity,

Vietnam—two decades of wanton inhumanity,
Invading despite purporting to respect sovereignty,
Poisoning with Napalm and Agent Orange, committing the My Lai atrocity,
Tricky Dicky opened up China whilst orchestrating the Watergate burglary,
'Law and Order' candidate, common theme, of justice making a mockery,
Defeated, disgraced and humiliated—the greatest military,
Public losing faith in the presidency,
Though the war and Nixon ended up on the wrong side of history,
Same mistakes soon repeated—not a nation given to collective self-reflectivity,
National Guard shooting kids unarmed on the campus of Kent State University,
Then eleven days later the police at Jackson State, Mississippi,
No reckoning as to if violence is inherent in the national psyche,

For nearly half a century, Roe v. Wade gave women bodily autonomy,
Until the advent of the Supreme Court's conservative super majority,
A representative democracy where the apex court reflects neither demography,
The popular sentiment of most of the country,
Nor, on account of life-time appointments, has accountability,

'*...government is the problem*' Reagan decried vehemently,
Whilst Reaganomics increased the national debt triply,

Techno-utopianism—we were sold a fantasy by Silicon Valley,
That the personal computer and then the Internet and every smart doohickey,
Would enhance our minds preternaturally,
Free our thoughts and individuality digi-democratically,
Make life and work easy futuristically,
Instead entertainment stupefyingly,
Social media depressingly,
Email and notifications pinging pesteringly,

Work and distraction now dog me inescapably,
In a digital dystopia where dangerously,
Dis and misinformation misleadingly,
In karmic circularity,
'Stole' the 2016 and 2024 elections from reasonability,

When the Iron Curtain rusted irreparably,
And the Berlin Wall fell portentously,
The end of the Cold War gave impetus fervently,
As McDonald's opened up in Moscow triumphally,
That democracy so fair and right—'twas time opportune to export it internationally,
Whilst gerrymandering at home to exclude the black and brown minority,

Because of Rodney King, systemic racism and chronic police brutality,
The justice system cornered itself into having to find OJ not guilty,

The right-wing couldn't stand 'Slick Willy',
Nor as time would prove Hillary,
So they threw at him not the book but the blue dress of Monica Lewinsky,
Impeaching him for infidelity,
But the back of him they didn't see—'cause, stupid, it's the economy,
21 to buy a beer, only 18 to buy an AR-15 and go on a school shooting spree,
But other than the obvious—banning guns—any remedy,
From arming teachers to droning on disingenuously,
About mental health to better windows, doors and locks absurdly,

'One man, one vote'—guarantor of representativity,
Gore v. Bush, besides the court's obvious partiality,
Electoral College Trumping the popular vote—unrepresentative perversity,

9/11 gravely scarring national tragedy,
That left the nation with PTSD,
But invading Iraq, attrition in Afghanistan only elongating and spreading the misery,

Tarnishing the victims' memory,
Weakening the country's standing and global moral authority,

Politicians playing to the gallery,
Insisting that Islam is a religion of peace publicly,
Then why block the building of a mosque near the former WTC?

If '*They hate us for our freedoms...*', is it not the terrorists who win unwittingly,
When with the Patriot Act and the Department of Homeland Security,
We retract and infringe on our hallowed freedoms reflexively?

White guy mass shooter—troubled loner; blame the breakdown of the family,
Non-white perpetrator—then surely:
Global Islamic terrorism rearing its head evilly,

Hurricane Katrina as it ravaged the Big Easy,
Proved that here even natural disasters kill on the basis of racial identity,

Same-sex marriage and marijuana legalization finally,
Depending of course between which lines you find yourself within arbitrarily,
In a country that can never agree—wouldn't expect anything differently,
'United' always was and more and more is used euphemistically,

Hollywood to the writing industry running out of creativity,
Besides, it takes sophisticate audiences to appreciate originality,
So no money in fiction—they turn to reality,
But Keeping up with the Kardashians = WWE,
Nothing more scripted than 'Reality' TV,

When the first black president was elected it was an inevitability,
That the retaliation would be rabid and reactionary,
That he was named Barack Hussein Obama along with his eloquent oratory,
Ivy league education and elite reputation though used as fodder cynically,

Exposed somewhat by the 'Birther' mendacity,
And the 'Tan Suit' ludicrous controversy,
It was really his race which made some white folk uneasy if not downright queasy,
His election's first retaliatory political tremor—the Tea Party,
Ultimately its blowback Trumpism and the MAGA calamity,

Obama got Osama—Zero Dark Thirty,
But 'founded' ISIS according to his nemesis—tweeter in chief of conspiracy,

Culture war stoked by Fox News and Info Wars talking head 'punditry',
Where in a post-fact anti-truth mediascape the preposterous inanity:
Pizzagate to Hunter Biden's laptop to Benghazi,
'Stop the Steal', it was a false flag at Sandy Hook Elementary,
All this can be passed off sans journalistic responsibility,
With Cronkitesque anchorman's solemnity,
To a degree,
Goebbels could only dream of and Orwell exaggerate in allegory,

Black Lives Matter and Me Too solid of substance, necessary and timely,
But their just missions compromised mortally,
By gender identity politics and woke social justice warrior baloney,
Which only gives ammunition to right-wing malarkey,
Far Left feeding Alt-Right in a downward death dance spirally,
Polar opposites, sworn enemies with one striking commonality:
Their world-views constructed by specious sophistry,

White working-class and poor, Bible thumping evangelicals, the rural backwoodsy,
Identifying with a big city 'billionaire', pussy-grabber, two-time divorcee,
Showboating his gaudy, gold-plated luxury,
Never did an honest day's work in his life and paid-off porn star Stormy,
Whose daughter makes him horny,
Claims he's self-made but inherited millions from daddy,
A twice impeached convicted felon re-elected convincingly,

To '...*preserve, protect and defend the Constitution...*' the very one against which he,
Fomented an insurrection treasonously,

Ivermectin and drinking bleach touted as Covid cures seriously,
Cast as the devil incarnate genial Dr. Fauci,
The 'China Virus' blamed on 5G,
The world including anti-vaxxers saved by the evil pharmaceutical industry,
But only because big government took matters into its own hands decisively,
But even bring up universal healthcare—you're a commie,
'Obamacare' considered too far left counterintuitively,
By guess who—many a right-leaning beneficiary,
So with Medicare and Medicaid do it half-heartedly,
And spend more than any other country only to have worse outcomes irrationally,

Long lockdowns over-reaction, retrospectively,
For if nothing else they made for the perfect petri dish from which infectiously,
Grew QAnon and many an other bizarre conspiracy theory,
Anti-lockdown protestors demanding their freedoms back sometimes violently,
Didn't know that the freedom from work would veer their minds so insanely,

Kneeling on the neck of one black man murderously,
Half the nation incensed indignantly,
And when another kneels during the Star Spangled Banner defiantly,
The other half incensed almost as fiercely,

World leader in AI—tech with apocalyptic potentiality,
But falling behind abysmally,
In tech that can save the planet from climate Armageddon—renewable energy,
Like every other big issue and non-issue seemingly,
Politicized and of course beholden to the corporate lobby,
In and out of the Paris Accords—a revolving door lack of policy continuity,
Depending on whether (R) or (D),
Follows the occupier of the White House—nothing anymore done bi-partisanly,

When it comes to book bans and 'Don't Say Gay' unconstitutionally,
Furor over Critical Race Theory to transphobia and fear of grooming baselessly,
The finger is pointed blamingly,
At the lack of education of the redneck and hillbilly,
But then what of the anti-free speech duplicity,
The cancel culture witch-hunt on the quad of the 'liberal' erudite Ivy,
Anti versus pseudo intellectualism undoubtedly,
A theme in national life typically,

Biggest funder of the UN whose General Assembly,
Has voted, time and again, overwhelmingly,
Demanding Israel ends its 'unlawful presence' in occupied Palestinian territory,
And censured it for egregious human rights violations unequivocally,
But also being Israel's biggest benefactor both militarily and financially,
Means being its biggest supporter, sympathizer and apologist necessarily,

Biden gaffes galore and à la McConnell freezes frequently,
So he's forced to step down reluctantly,
But Harris despite being a schoolgirl relatively,
It must be voiced though politically incorrectly,
Her youth couldn't compensate for her color and gender electorally,
So back to the 'very stable genius'—three and a half years younger only,
Who aces cognitive tests of great difficulty,
'*Person, woman, man, camera, TV*' his flubs and fumbles famously,
The staple of late-night comedy,
Still considering itself a young country—a youthocracy,
From president to the Senate—very much a gerontocracy,

Left the Old World behind determined that here there will be no aristocracy,
Founded on dethroning monarchy,
But ever since enthroning whether Camelot or the cult of celebrity,
Here the rich are made not born—this is supposed to be a meritocracy,
Where pulling yourself up from your own bootstraps anyone can be wealthy,

A mythos serving well the 1% billionaire plutocracy,
A lone shrill voice screaming into the void, Bernie,
And like the first merry-go-round of morons—Herschel Walker to Rudy Giuliani,
Soon Trump 2.0's cavalcade of clowns will usher in a kakistocracy,
The real power behind the throne a tech titan oligarchy,

But though your fast-food saddles me with pounds and pounds of obesity,
Your entertainment addles me with stupidity,
Your workaholism riddles my mind and body with stress and anxiety,
Your chemicals cause my ills and your cures push me to bankruptcy,
Your optimism and Dream unfulfills leaving my life meaningless and empty,
Your crass creed selling cheap thrills uglifies beauty with Vegasesque vulgarity,
Your interventions and invasions spills into endless death, destruction and catastrophe,
Your rapacious consumerism kills Mother Earth heedless that there's no Planet B,

Though you're the Third World in the First World and vice versa mind-flucktuatingly,
And it is you who's the real riddle inside an enigma wrapped in a mystery,
For all you have done for the world and me,
'Murica, you're one huge countrydictory, but oh how I love thee!

Glutton Free

I wish food were scarcer so that my tummy was always a tad empty,
For then whatever I could get my greedy hands on I'd eat aplenty,

Not relentlessly wrestling the 'Battle of the Bulge',
Not stressed about cardiac arrest—no such thing as to over-indulge,

I'd toss the salad bar for some fried Mars bars,
Scoop with my finger peanut butter jars,

And best of all, to my growling tum-tum,
Every morsel will taste infinitely more yum-yum,

Yes, I know, I know Grandma, I should be grateful for this plentitude,
Starving African kids in their wildest dreams couldn't imagine all this food,

Though it may seem like First World nonsense:
Calorie conscious equals a guilty conscience,

I can see it now: me a kid in a candy store licking every lolly,
Not checking sugar, sodium and glycemic index before shoving it in my trolly,
Who cares about fat, trans or poly?
And none of this gluten free folly,
I'd just eat to my fill and be a whole lot more jolly!

Dormnation

Thirty years I will pay my dues to this place—but a restless bed to sleep,
It keeps me up at night—can I manage its exorbitant upkeep!?

With its spaciousness grows my emptiness it seems,
Whatever happened to my freewheeling footloose dreams?

Sigh—but with the Joneses I must compete,
My manicured lawn must be OCD neat,
Neighborly small-talk I must bleat,
Forcing a grin dinner guests I must greet,
At Halloween and Christmas, I must adorn it with frills, bells and whistles replete,

But sometimes when these four expansive walls hem in around my feet,
Anxious my net worth will crash my self-worth in a 2008 repeat,
I wanna give it all up—stop worrying for the interest of Wall Street,
I feel even couch-surfing would be more of a presidential suite,
My home wherever the wind blows; my hearth passion's heat,

That's just being silly!
I must grow my home equity—I can't throw it all away willy-nilly!

Besides, paying off my mortgage is my magnum opus Herculean deed,
So, proud of my house—I am, I am—indeed!
My life story, well, is my expensive dormitory—I guess I must concede,
The American Dream: Heaven on 'burb? Or to dormnation doth it lead?

Chooser Loser

As true of people as of things, I wish for few—not for many,
Not only the bad, this goes as much for the good and the very,
For from the aisles to the aisle, the avalanche of choice doth bury,
Tis indeed a formidable modern adversary,

'Cause of billions of profiles vying in the digital abyss,
To way too many brands of every that and this,
That which I have I can't behold in bliss,
For from all that I have missed—a relentless niggling hiss,

And that's not all, fittingly there's more,
The 'Paradox of Choice' not just a mere modern chore,
For modernity to 'Live my best life' doth implore,
For others sure, but 'Live and let live' for me it doth deplore,
So down to every trivial decision to ward-off FoMO, with perfectionism keeping score,
I agonize, obsess, finick, nit-pick, hair-split—I over-think at least twice before,

But let's face it—I'm no rational decision making pro,
In fact, anyone like that I don't even know,
Even behavioral economists with Nobel Prizes to show,
Confide that their own advice often they do not follow!

I'm just an amateur chooser,
Who, whichever I settle for, ends up feeling like the loser.

Love Laborer

For my lover,
Inspired I'd write her a sensuous sonnet, I'd pluck her a baroque flower,
Waltz with her 'neath a champagne monsoon shower,

Over her beatific beauty—I can't help but swoon,
A longing lullaby croon,
Her serene sleep seduces me to snuggle and spoon,
I'd propose to her under the blessings of the opportune moon,

But the problem is,
When I feel enforced to do all this,
And on top of which to communicate absolutely everything without a miss,

Hallmark cards peddling cornball troubadour verse,
Relationship gurus badgering to converse,
Whilst influencer quacks formulaic date-night tropes disburse,
Can you blame me if to the burden of love as work I've grown averse?

Inevitably then, as with my employer or boss, of course with them I can't let it show,
Upon my lover to whom this canned obligation I owe,
Seeds of resentment I begin to sow,

So we bicker and tiff,
Each other's fault—as if,

In the heat of argument neither can be expected to stop and think,
That inexorably capitalism the hitherto consummate in a blink,
Doth transmogrify into yet another mere alienating job, all the while trying to hoodwink,
The worker into simultaneously loving his alienation—this is its devious doublethink,

So, what once was a labor of love,
I am now a laborer of love hereof.

9 to Supine

Tis a curious thing about drudgery,
How it leads in whichever way, shape or form to gluttony,

Alarm clock on snooze,
Monday blues,
Bumper-to-bumper—my shit I'm already about to lose,
Only to open up email slews,
Meeting after meeting—there pointlessness bemuse,
All the while my boss's ego I gotta schmooze,
Repeat in reverse the traffic abuse,

So many of us hating what we do,
Yet we soldier through,

Of course, having to do what we'd rather not,
One thing after another with all we've got,
Drains willpower a lot,
'Ego-depletion' psychologists call this rot,

So, at the end of another long groundhog day,
And when we exhale TGIF: '*Thank god it's Friday*',
Our life force sapped away,
We are left passive prey,

Nothing left with which to think,
Some shop till they drop, binge eat, watch and drink,
In debt and fat and smut they sink,
While others robotically continue working till they breach their brink,
Both barely noticing before they're back on the treadmill in an 8-hour blink,

9 to 5—who are we kidding? More like 9 to supine,
So watch out for your will's insidious decline,
That makes you seek the stupefaction of your mind,
Oh, and keep an eye on your bulging behind.

Till Debt

Debt tis not mere money borrowed,
Tis my life pawned—forever my brow furrowed,

During my ever-lengthening working hours,
And on the weekends where oft my finances further sours,
Even when I'm frolicking with friends and lovers,
The specter of debt night and day hovers,

That background noise that's infernally hissin' is my anxiety arisen,
I can suppress it but when what's 'mine' really isn't—it won't listen,
I'm indentured in a monthly repayment prison,

But telling me to live within my means—now that's ascetic in the extreme,
Don't you dare blaspheme my American Dream,

My spendthrift binging may prolong my sentence—but hey!
There's another credit card on the way,
So I'll be A-Ok,
And I'll show you—for next time too I'll put nothing away,

I'll keep bending over bankwards,
Serving big interests with my interest—saving up?—so backwards!

Willfully ignorant that I'm on 'borrowed time',
Until I find that the financial system has Madoff with my hard-earned dime,

And without technically committing a crime,
Has inevitably pulled-off the next sub-prime,

Sometimes though I do find it funny,
How I'm browbeaten into being a self-denier except when it comes to spending money,

Eat less, drink less, sit less, scroll less, watch less,
Work more, sleep more, run more and breathe more to destress,
But BUY, BUY, BUY—you deserve the best so there's no such thing as excess,

It figures, I suppose,
Lest the holy of holies—economic growth—slows,
Which at this stage of capitalism, everyone knows,
Shall come to pass unless consumer spending interminably grows,

Either way, I'm a modern citisumer—I've been indoctrinated from the start,
Whether I can afford it or not—even if it's not financially smart,
To keep filling up my shopping cart,
To honor a solemn vow: that until from this life I depart,
Though it may be bad for my peace-of-mind and my heart,
Mortgages, student loans, credit cards—till debt do we part.

Exorcise

Ten thousand steps,
Nor endless crunches and reps,
Just like diet fads,
For your average lard ladies and lads,
Offer no more than a false glimmer,
Of making them fitter, trimmer or slimmer,
So the nutritionist to the Peloton pusher to the fitness guru,
Would do well to learn from the psychologist a thing or two,

Exercise implies by definition to comfort now forsake for our future's sake,
But you see, from the time we wake,
All our energies and worries we dedicate,
To bend the vagaries of our fate,
To our covetousness sate,
From how to pay for our kids' college to our 401Ks to the state of our prostate,
And even what we're gonna leave as our estate,
In other words, from our now we beg, steal and borrow—
We sacrifice today at the altar of a better tomorrow,
So my weary body and soul at the end of the day,
On the couch just wants to lay,

For evolution many millennia before the modern calorie inundation,
With survival at stake had to balance the energy equation,
By preprogramming me toward energy conservation,
So what I naturally seek out is instant gratification,

Not more toil and self-exploitation,
To laboriously accumulate distant compensation,

Enter play:
From whence I lay to get off my fat ass the best way,
Why? Well it all comes down to this—
The psychology of bliss,
For when we play, it's the moment we revel in and in which we stay,
As opposed to transacting 'now' away,
In exchange for hoped for reward far faraway,
From this very fact about play it should ensue,
That unlike exercise we needn't have to drone on and drill it in anew,
Remember as kids play is all we knew?
We just need to remind ourselves how caution to the wind we threw,
The future no issue,
Not on leaden legs but on breezy hearts—oh how we flew!
As much as it is of happiness—how true:
That fitness too as a bonus doth best accrue,

So 'work'ing-out over play—the more we emphasize,
Counter-productively, the more the average Joe we disincentivize,
Mechanized ergo boring and necessarily painful—of course we despise,
We'd rather do anything else than work reprise!
Turned-off—the couch potato cannot rise,
Instead, pigging-out on the likes of burgers and fries,
We binge on screens which feed us escapist lies,

So this anti-natural commandment whose virtues modernity doth so sermonize,
This excruciation called exercise,
Its pre-eminence over play let's exorcise.

Mindfoolness

'Stay in the moment' is all the rage,
Stalk each and every thought from conception through its every life stage,
Investigate its provenance, unpack its repercussions, how it makes you feel gauge,
Preaches the modern self-help sage,
As he hawks his snake oil wrapped in the aura of a mystic buddhistic package,

But don't they know that the anxiety epidemic which plagues today,
Is in small part nay,
Brought on by the evangelization of meta-cognition they purvey?
Which, hitherto, was the mental price only philosophers had to pay,
For you see, it morphs soon into fruitless over-thinking for the lay,
Unbearable on their shoulders it doth weigh,

Whereas the philosopher's mind,
Its very calling is to be inclined,
To hone in on the most critical questions facing humankind,
And cogitate upon that which man dare not leave unopined,
Thereby, the greater good justifies the philosopher's mental anguish and grind,
The lay, conversely, are inclined to be by a soppy solipsism entwined,

Not trenchant, useful nor creative muses,
The devil putting their over-wrought rumination to his own uses,
Each a modern chronic over-thinker marooned to stew in his own mental juices,

Wherefrom a masochistic self-indulgence takes grip,
Which is wont to let rip,
At the mere sight of the pettiest molehill's tip,
And which like all self-indulgence makes for an instantly gratifying short-term trip,
But which often your long-term best-interests in the bud nip,

Thus, contrarily to the gurus whom about mindfulness's magic sermonize,
The polar opposite I would advise:
To relish the moment—get over yourself and let go!
Allow yourself to drift away into a state psychologists call 'Flow',
A time out of mind—not a care nor woe,
A supra-conscious fugue state of intense nothingness that goes both fast and slow,
The beatitude of gratitude the afterglow,
I know, tis the very anti-thesis of trying too hard with little but angst to show,
Give it a go for mindfoolness really does blow.

Fat Blaming

Love the body you're in—don't stand for no fat-shaming,
Yeah but if you're overweight (or for that matter under) don't be blaming,
When '*Who's that eye candy!?*'—nobody be exclaiming,

See, evolutionary psychology dictates—whether we like it or no,
That bodily attractiveness is all about the female waist-to-hip golden ratio,
And the male muscular V-shaped torso,

So it really shouldn't leave you agape,
When say the pear and apple are not as hot as the hourglass shape,
For as markers of reproductive fitness, as opposed to being over-weight,
They give our genes their best chances to propagate,

And, though it's beyond doubt's shadow,
That tis your right to be a twiggy or a fatso,
From this it does not follow,
That tis also your right to be deemed a 'smoke show',

As much as obesity, thin-skintitis a modern disease,
Its etiology can be traced back to when a parasite called wokeness did seize,
Liberalism by both its mind and testes,

An ideology which is almost as antagonistic to truth and reason,
As the conspiracy lunacies which drove the Jan. 6th insurrectionists to treason,

Egalitarians really should hold to '*You shouldn't judge a book by its cover*',
And '*Beauty is in the eye of the lover*',
For beyond this without a leg to stand when they sputter,
When nonsense such as '*All bodies are beautiful*' they utter,
It's only their intellectual credentials which suffer,

Moreover, when the obese you so appease,
Don't delude yourself into thinking that you're doing them any favors, please,

If you do have a genetic predilection to an unfavorable metabolism,
Down a path toward your health's detriment thinking it altruism,
Though it's mostly out of self-serving sentimentalism,
How does it help you if I enable and cheer you on, mainly with my clicktivism?

Look, if you've got nothing nice to say, it's often best if you say nothing at all,
So fat shaming—no biggie—yes, out we should call,
But when you get your expectations all out of whack,
Skinny, hot or fat—this does not change the facts, despite all your flack,
Instead, fat blaming on the fat fires back.

Number Crunched

Tis not English nor even Mandarin, as you might expect,
Which has become the dominant modern dialect,
No, that's numbers and stats,
Figures though not necessarily facts,

Credit twelve years of grueling schooling,
For this improved literacy in numeracy,
And thank computers for crunching ones and zeros so cheaply,
And making them available ubiquitously and presenting them so neatly,

So of course we value our life in years,
Our self-worth by the net worth of our peers,
And the likes and followers which on our social media feeds appears,
Our problems by our credit card and mortgage arrears,
And body fat, blood sugar and pressure measure our fears,

But, it's inevitable and clear,
That there's a spillover defect here,

See, the more fluent and hence possessed by numbers we get,
It becomes that much easier to execute our instinctive social animal preset:
To compare—which we are too often wont to do until we are beset,

So with our previous selves and who we want to be,
And with everyone else, obviously,

We do more comparing almost unwittingly,
Which for discontentment is the recipe,

But from this malady's core,
Where we compulsively keep score,
Stems suffering much more,

'*There are lies, damned lies and then there are statistics!*',
So metrics can play reductionist mind tricks:
They induce you to reduce every quality divine,
Into some quantity profane and anodyne,
And when you do, you can say au revoir,
To the je ne sais quoi,

But that's not even the end of it,
Our obsession with analytics which makes us fidget about every decimal and digit,
Given that to modern life stress is anyways endemic,
Exacerbates it by being so pedantic,
It's negatively synergistic,
We're being penny wise but pound idiotic,

So from the frigid digits, the number stumper over which you're hunched,
Lunge up and live before you are number crunched!

iRony Store

Conceived in the Enlightenment zeitgeist at human thought's height,
Individualism that hard-won right,
Which soon took a turn quite:
From the concession that an inalienable capaciousness is each man's birthright,
To this modern mutation into a duty wherein everyone is obliged to delight,

Now being an average-joe,
A big NO-NO!
But here's the thing, though,
Not everyone is a rare rainbow,
And so the hitherto couldn't-care-less schmo,
Is saddled with a burden nouveau:
To himself he must prove and to others show,
That he is as unique as a flake of snow,

Cue the marketers' intro:
'*We've got some magic beans for that!*'—just try this branded gizmo,
From there the intoxicating promises overflow,
'Have it Your Way'... 'Because You're Worth it'—you're no Jane nor John Doe,
'Think Different' because 'Impossible is Nothing'—purchase so,
That unlike the bleating sheeple that blindly follow,
You'll stand out from the stale status quo,

Cuckamamie contradiction, although,
For like johns patronizing the same corporate bordello,

Clients of the same hookers who each other pretend to not know,
'*I'm unique!*' though each is coached to crow,
Since at the same convenience mart all shop for individuality—hey presto!

They are even more the same than before,
They are all loyal customers of the iRony Store.

Musturbator

Mental health is all the rage,
Pills to self-care to working through your woes on the couch of the modern 'sage',
But none of this will but momentarily assuage,
For what actually ails you is of your own making and that of your age,
Tis that you have locked yourself in a cage,
In which a self-cannibalistic war against yourself you wage,

See beyond that which nature takes care of via instinctive survival thrusts,
Each age has 'Shoulds' which are wont to become 'MUSTS',
Why? Well, because man innately for more and more insatiably lusts,

Axiomatically, the thing with a 'MUST',
Is that it is not an option just,
It has to be done or else!—you will self-combust!

And it is fair to suppose,
That as history flows,
Not only do the 'MUSTS' change but also their number grows,
For humanity's ever accumulating mastery more 'Coulds' bestows,
Which soon mature into 'Shoulds'—it's that self-same lust which doth predispose,
And then ruling as 'MUSTS' their wills over us they impose,

You must put eighty hours in with a grin,
You must spend time with kith and kin,
You must your retirement savings begin,

You must take ups and downs on the chin,
You must moisturize your skin,
You must crush it at the gym so you can remain thin...
And that's just the bare min!

It's just too many grenades to juggle,
Anyone can be forgiven if under this do-or-'die' pressure they buckle,

Tragicomically, definitely the abettor if not the perpetrator—
Psychologists—the perfect coinage doth cater,
When to your own mental well-being you become an obsessive-compulsive traitor,
The shrink nomenclator labels you a MUSTurbator.

Atrophy

You CANNOT do,
Whatever you set your mind to,
Hear me out—tis only to unburden you,
Tis not as a contrarian I spew,
Not to rabble-rouse I argue,

They say the road to hell is paved with good intentions,
Very true here for the well-meaning have given you false pretensions,

For only the rare few are truly great, and even they not at everything,
Usually, just at one thing,
Most are above average at something,
And some, I'm afraid, are good at nothing,

Yet true as it is none of this,
Should keep us from relishing life's wonder and glory and bliss,
For within us whatever isn't or is as enraptured witnesses life we needn't miss,

And, here's how you know where you fit in,
When you're meant for something, pretty much the moment you begin,
There's a consummate ease to your performance therein,
There's much less fret, frustration and chagrin,
Than for the unsuited slogger for whom it's an uphill no-win,
So if you're the latter, shrug 'So what?', take it on the chin,
Save yourself some suffering keeping in mind with a grin,
Hobbyists have the most fun so give it a dilettante's spin,

But alas long before the starting gun,
I was setup to fail before the race had even begun,
By being declared a winner—regardless of the outcome Number 1,

What did you expect!? Obviously, from there my 'hoop dreams' grew,
What's worse, I felt entitled to them coming true,

If I took up the violin,
I expected to be the next Yehudi Menuhin,
I expected to grow tall to play ball, and be like Mike—dunking,
I expected to think different and conceive like Steve—industry disrupting,

Hook, line and sinker I had taken the bait and swallowed the 'blue pill',
That had been sold to me by the likes of Oprah and Dr. Phil,

But when the 10,000-hour prescription of Gladwell,
Didn't turn out so well—
Just another bill of goods with a pseudoscientific oversell,
To the jagged, unforgiving terrain of reality with a rude thud I fell,
For contrary to what they had insisted to their vapid wares sell,
I really wasn't all that swell!

The self-esteem movement, that has long since lost intellectual steam,
Also conveniently left out another pivotal thing it does seem:
Talent or no, whether you win or home you go,
Depends, than on you, often more so,
On whether the world says 'YES' or 'NO',

Learning all this the hard way, I've made up my mind, you see,
To what the naturals and greats create partake with awe and glee,
For this rests much easier on my psyche,
I won't let a meaningless grade school trophy,
My contentment atrophy.

Hipster Puritan

I wake up to kale smoothies,
I never fall asleep watching indy movies,

I listen to vintage vinyl,
I ride a retro cycle,

I'm anti-global warming,
I'm pro-organic farming,

I ask for your preferred pronoun,
I believe systemic racism keep black and brown down,

I cancel Islamophobia and Antisemitism against the Jew,
I'm for women's right to choose and I march for 'Me Too',

Cultural appropriation must stop,
And of course—old white men must no longer be on top,

But don't get me wrong—you'll never see me drop acid or hug a tree,
Though my sartorial irony sometimes has pretensions to be,
I'm neither beatnik nor hippie!

Mine is no counter-culture suffused with mystic spirituality,
'The Man' has been good to me in actuality,
So I put in 70 hours a week,
At my 401(k) take a regular peek,

Not far from Woodstock,
I invest, I own stock,

Stress mitigation is why I don yoga pants,
Gentrification syncs snugly with my career and financial plans,

No adventure nor bacchanalia that'd my life goals waylay askew,
In lieu only a healthful kombucha brew,
Just so I can look at myself in the mirror political paraphernalia will do,
And for my rebel credentials—perhaps a badass piercing and/or tattoo,

It's not about changing the world, see,
Though 'basic' is pretty much a slur in my community,
Basically—it's all about me,
My whole shtick is the answer to the question, contrived craftily:
How can I revolt innocuously?
How can I be a straight-and-narrow square revolutionary?

But as much as I try with my wry beard and careful-carelessness chic to belie,
I'm just a conformist contorting to deny,

I'm 'woke' enough to know,
If I didn't with all these affectations have to put on a show,
Method act a persona oh so faux,
I could give back way more—not hypocritically perpetuate the status quo,

Hipster—I play the part,
But I'm a puritan at heart,
Now I have to go save the world—my vegan fast I must start.

Grumble Brag

'I wish I could make it...
But my schedule just won't permit',
'I'm up to my neck...
Ah! I just wanna walk away—what the heck!',
'I'm so busy, gee...
If only I had more time to be free!',
What you really mean is '*Look at me!:*
I'm needed, I'm wanted, I'm too important to lie dormant',

Well, from the other side of the divide,
Here's a tit-for-tat grumble-brag comeback uttered with equal pride,

The freedom I speak of is a blank canvas, an expansiveness,
That only potentials an infiniteness,
But at first it's just emptiness,
Dark and stark,
Waiting for you—its big bang, its sun—to spark,

The hardest part?
Is, of course, to start,
Hence why even that freedom from serfdom so rare,
That the rat-race doth only here-and-there spare,
Can at first stare,
Be racked with banal boredom even debilitating despair,

And, even when you manage to start,
Remember—the untravelled path can have neither guideposts, map nor chart,
Indeed, it is those who seek this in their heart,
Who make the best fist of the art,

Making it up as you go along poking around in the dark,
Up many a wrong tree as you bark,
'Busy' bodies on the straight-and-narrow will sling arrows of snark,
Some on you may even narc,

What you'll need is neither to heed the wise men nor heel to the sheep's bleat,
But to carefully cultivate the ability to listen quietly to your inner beat,
And to this—your own drumbeat—resolutely march your feet,

That's the grumble so there's the grief, but if you take the leap,
Here's what you reap:
Like a Moses atop Mt. Maslow—the light through the mainstream smokescreen,
You see the hitherto unseen,
For you are he who has never before been,

And the brag?
Well, when freedom's riches you bag,
You can make the aforesaid—'My Way'— grumble-brag,
Knowing full well that only very few have your swag.

Binge Worker

'It's quitting time! Woohoo! The rest of the day is all mine!',
Whoa, easy there buddy—I'm fooling myself if I think I can daily resign,
For as a cog in late capitalism here's my fate and thine,

That holy grail: more and more with less and less—with which we are possessed,
That hankering from every second to the very utmost wrest,
That striving to forever better my best,
This all-consuming hegemonic quest,
Tis easier-said-than-done to its echoing behest:
To preachify- *'At work's door leave then enjoy and rest'*,

Like the drummer who practices all day,
Give me any old semblance of a stick—my will has little say,
Repetition-compulsion over me holds sway,
To the gym—to-do list ticking, Blinkist skimming away,
Working-out to productivity podcasts trying to burn-off that sorbet,
Check step-count on Fitbit then on the scale my self-worth weigh,
Efficiently assembly-line healthy dinner, institute sleep hygiene protocol then lay,
Whether on weekends or on the rarely availed holiday,
Or getting down to business with my bae:
Output over play,
Not Carpe Diem—'*Seize the day*'—hell nay,
But—the sun is always shining so of each and every moment I must make hay,
Time management—modern ethos not cliché,
Most everyone's really now Type A,

Living our 'Best lives' in a self-exploitative way,
And like all religions when man dare not obey,
Anxiety and guilt enter the fray,
So if from productivity I sin and stray,
If I shirk the great calling of today:
'*Every moment and day thou must slay*',
My conscience the price must pay,
But unlike the creeds of yesterday,
Tis not god but—worse—tis myself I betray,
I am a binge worker—I work therefore I pray.

Existentialitis

Better education and nutrition,
The Enlightenment and science triumphing over dogma and superstition,
Complex and stimulating environments demanding more of cognition,
Even the Internet in its original noble mission,

All allies which together actualize—
The 'Flynn Effect': as nations get richer, average IQs rise,
But have we paid a hefty mental price for becoming 'wise'?

True, Third World life is rife,
With rancor and hunger, disease and strife,

But despite of this,
Their ignorance still affords them mental bliss,

For the big questions do not so much as occur to the fools,
Besides, they do not have the tools,
To wind their minds in metaphysical over-thinking spools,

And over that which they must worry,
They have God and Gods to feel sorry,

But for those in 'the know' the depression epidemic is endemic,
They face every day the age-old philosopher's fate so tragic,

What is the meaning, the purpose of this all?
Am I no more than just another carbon-based life-form? I feel so small!

How can I create my own meaning?
I feel into the abyss of nihilism I'm careening,

The curse of intelligence, then, is no trifle,
Existentialitis: A strain of affluenza in my modern mind viral.

Nuts Allergy

From peanuts to PTSD,
To BPD, NPD, MDD etc., ADD the ubiquitous ADHD,
Everybody has something nowadays seemingly,
So much so that I self-diagnose me with every variety of malady,
I know my cousin was on the spectrum— definitely he's got ASD,
So maybe... or is it just my OCD!?
Either way, undoubtedly, I need therapy—most likely CBT,

Though, in moments of sanity,
Increasingly a rarity,
I do ponder if this is all a pathologization pandemic absurdly gone OTT,
Creating a 'generalized' anxiety disorder (GAD),

But the experts assure,
With a certainty cocksure,
That in the past let alone finding a cure,
These disorders were not yet discovered or so obscure,
That they went undiagnosed or underdiagnosed for sure,

Hmm, this doesn't quite convince somehow,
Me thinks it's got more to do with the zeitgeist—the spirit of now,
And individualism the creed that modernity doth unreservedly avow,

Where I am the sun, where everything revolves around me,
It stands to reason that I am more than prone to be,

Obsessive about the upkeep of me the alpha-and-omega, wouldn't you agree?
From there it takes but a short leap to see,
Why to make a mountain out of every molehill the pedantic proclivity,

Doctor's orders: self-indulgently wallow in my BED:
Binge Eating Disorder—but what's really devouring my life, the real pathology,
Is the solipsism of modernity, and that's so SAD,
For which there's no therapy nor remedy at the pharmacy, prescription nor OTC,
It's nuts—me is the allergy.

Self-Yelp

At modernity's behest,
I've learnt a little too well to get each and everything off my chest,

Not a trifle do I stifle,
Not an itch on which I do not snitch,

Now, if your step-dad watched you undress,
Or growing-up your family was a dysfunctional mess,
Or if you feel depressed, anxious or are under immense stress,
Yes—most certainly—do not repress,
For to convalesce it is essential to decompress,

But far short of the pathological,
And even the sub-clinical,
We've become hypochondriacs of the trivial—which to mental health is inimical,

See, words cannot only express feelings,
They can create them—they can plant seedlings,
And they can exaggerate—from molehills make mountainous meaning,
This, in turn, can cause yet more internal bleeding,

For words have the power to make the amorphous psychically concrete,
And lay layer upon layer of brick on a bare-bones foundation petty and petite,
Until a mighty edifice is complete,

À la a tiny mole or other such 'imperfection',
Which may very well only be so in your perception,
Which appears only to grow with each obsessive inspection,
Which if you go under the plastic surgeon's knife for 'correction',
May end up a botched eyesore thus drawing more attention in your direction,

Catharsis expropriated from trauma and grief—its appropriate sphere,
This I fear,
For now that to voice my every minor mal-feeling I have the 'all-clear',
And since from my therapist to my lover to my peer,
All are obliged to lend an empathetic ear—
More wallowing blears,
On more shoulders to cry on just means more self-yelp tears.

Feelosophy

My mind was wondering just the other day,
About all the things modernity has to say,
When something struck me in an indelible way,
About almost every aphorism and every cliché,

I riffled through proverbs and maxims of yore and even the recent past,
'Twas plain to see the stark contrast,

'*Just be yourself*' you're a superstar,
'*Embrace your flaws*' because '*You are perfect just the way you are*',

'*Think positive*' because '*Everything happens for a reason*' so '*Never quit*',
'*You can do anything if you only set your mind to it*',

'*You miss 100% of the shots you don't take*',
'*YOLO: You only live once*' so of every day the most make,

'*Follow your dreams*' and '*Live every day like it's your last*',
'*The best is yet to come*' so leave behind the past—the possibilities are limitless and vast,

And '*Live, laugh, love*',
While doing all of the above,

That seminal kernel of truth, that edifying insight,
Has been superseded and marginalized out of sight,
By mawkishly pollyannish corny baloney feel-good shite,

Now if I were of a conspiratorial bent,
I would surely vent,
That this is all just cynical propaganda to manufacture consent,
A carrot of hope dangled to keep the rats running lest they relent,
To 'inspire' them to race faster to profit the One Percent,
Opium for the masses to keep them from growing malcontent,
Perhaps this is true in part,
But there's something more which goes as much to its heart,

Every creed its adherents to win and keep,
Must its believers by hook or by crook off their feet sweep,
It follows then that individualism too must supply its 'sheep',
With the requisite faith to keep taking the leap,
It's really not any more than this deep,

Individualism is modernity's avowed creed,
So it must do everything in its power to the individual's self-belief feed,
And his hope breed,
Ergo we shouldn't be surprised when it follows that salivating to succeed:
Feelosophy be its philosophy—mature individualism has decreed.

Disown Joy

The beauty, wonder and the joy of many a thing from house to car to gadget to toy,
And sometimes even the pretty girl and the handsome boy,
We all too often can scarcely enjoy,

For nary a moment to myself I permit,
To behold it even for a bit,
I must, I must have and own it!

Oft marketers' promises in our eyes glinting,
'*All that glitters is not gold*' not entering our thinking,
We presume than sipping better surely must be whole-hog drinking,

And herein,
Paying for greed—our sin,
The rot sets in,

Consider what ownership actually can add:
Control? Duration? Convenient access? Does it your ego pad?

But proud owner keep in mind,
Maintenance and protection—an onerous responsibility you may find,
For everything to rust and decline is inclined,
And only what's yours can be lost, need I remind?
What's more, by your acquisition you may be confined,
To explore other options—too late—on the dotted line you have signed,

You've invested so much you're in a resource bind,
And, even if it's a bad bargain, to let go of all you've already spent you're disinclined,

'Pluck'em—they'll smell sweeter', though ownership expediently proposes,
Many a time reality opposes,
Then tis it not wiser to stroll through the garden smelling all the roses?

Possession is nine-tenths of the law they say,
But of our contentment—no way!
In fact, our nerves it can fray,
Upon our peace of mind it can prey,

So sit back, enjoy—to own be coy,
For by owning you may disown joy.

Rich Bitch

Pop star, sports star, movie star,
Though up above us by far,
You still are,
You've got competition now from a new type of modern superstar,

On the playground we used to all wanna be like Mike,
Jordan or Jackson alike,
To fly from the free-throw line, to moonwalk—for the wild-eyed tyke,
'Twas magic, 'twas dreamlike,

But you know who kids nowadays lionize,
As much or even more than those we used to idolize?
Billionaires—and in hegemonic capitalism this should come as no surprise,
That tis the arch capitalist we apotheosize,

Musk, Bezos, Zuckerberg, Gates,
The very class the soon-to-be working stiff is better-off if he hates,

See when I didn't grow to be six-foot-six tall,
When, ha, Hollywood didn't call,
When after high school all I could do was flip burgers at the local mall,
It was obvious—I was not cut out to sing nor act nor play pro ball,

But that's the thing with patently talent derived fortune and fame,
You know it when you've got game,

And if like most you don't—there ain't no shame,
In at a more realistic job taking aim,

But in business all you need to strike it rich,
Is hard work, an idea and an irresistible sales pitch,
Or so it goes in the modern yarn in which,
Opportunity and luck are conveniently given the ditch,

So unlike in sports or entertainment or some such comparably long-shot field,
Well past where the daydream of youth its sway doth wield,
To harsh reality the working stiff still loathe to yield,

Indeed, many believe their grit and grindset,
Must the odds in their favor beget,
With globalization, of course, exporting this very American mindset,

To help the poor tax the 1% high,
But why,
When the moment you're about to join the ranks of the rich is nigh?

In fact, why organize, unionize, mobilize—waste time and money on any of that,
To uplift the socio-economic station you won't be long at?

Explains why too many of the poor like bugs against their own good go splat,
In favor of the vested interests of the oligarch and the plutocrat,
Vote Republican not Democrat!

Back when to the talented our fantasy wagons we used to hitch,
The socio-economic fallout was but a smidge: no more than the star did we enrich,
But now with the cult of the self-made billionaire the rich have made us their bitch.

Untertainment

There's less in the way of entertainment today,
Wait, '*WHAT!?*' you say,

How can this astounding assertion which so blatantly belies the eye test,
Nevertheless manifest?

Well, the argument's entire fundament,
Revolves around directness of intent,

See, for something to be entertaining it must arouse, stoke and engross,
Whether funny, fascinating or gross,

Now of all the myriad things which possess this ability,
Some are robbed of their virility,
If it comes to be known or believed that there's been a compromising of authenticity,

If the audience learns or feels the entertainers have strayed,
From the taken for granted 'way the game should be played',
The hallowed means via which to arouse, stoke and engross the attempt is made,
The potential actualization of entertainment is spayed:
Tis rendered impotent to arouse, stoke and engross—none are swayed,
And the audience is left feeling betrayed,

Sports provides the paradigmatic illustration:
Groweth the ardency of a belief or credence of an allegation,

That the action, score or result has been contrived by adulteration,
That it has been 'fixed' to serve a particular party's aspiration,
Or staged to puppeteer audience captivation,
Thereby forfeited is said sport's capacity for stimulation,
Roving eye-balls flee in search of genuine confrontation,
Die-hard fans up in arms with indignation,
Demand the purity of untampered competition's restoration,

Of course, none of this applies,
To fiction where tis expected that to the fabrication the audience is wise,
Their suspension of disbelief a prerequisite on which the creator relies,
To his reader, viewer or listener captivate and mesmerize,

And, here's the sting in the modern tale,
That leads to many an epic fail,

There's just so much money to be made,
If only the millions if not billions of eye-balls you can persuade,
And there's so much of tech and so many tricks with which to masquerade,
The temptation is too irresistible to be disobeyed,

So all and sundry from the documentary filmmaker to the journalistic muckraker,
The Guinness record breaker to your average picture taker,
The news anchor to the CEO wanker,
Pastor to podcaster,
Discovery Channel to the expert panel,
Politician to dietician,
Chef to influencer beautician,
Aspiration: wannabe 'steak'-less marketing magician,

Instrumentally and cynically selling-out what they do with eyes,
Fixated firmly on the prize,
Namely to eye-balls focalize,

Oh modern life, blinders on single-mindedly you go rip-roaring,
Where it doesn't belong fiction pouring,
With excessive exaggeration underscoring,
Taking too direct a route to entertain ignoring—
That it was the portrayal of truths and realities of which I was adoring,
Self-defeatingly—thanks to your attention whoring,
My interest has waned, my attention has gone exploring,
For your untertainment is quite boring.

Modern Regress

Barely done with kindergarten kids' parents' eyes on the future fix,
Already weighing their college picks,
First day at work but young man's,
Already making retirement plans,
From your twenties on goaded into taking prostate exams,
And annual mammograms,
Then electrocardiograms,

'*Qué será, será, whatever will be, will be...*',
Is quite the conspicuous absentee,
In the thought processes of modernity,
Which is quite the dual irony,
For firstly,
We are sermonized with self-help zealotry,
To doggedly 'Live in the moment' mindfully,
And secondly,
Whilst our personal futures exclusively,
We are moralized to plot, plan and prepare for painstakingly,
We obliviously,
Though, really willfully ignorantly,
Reign down upon ourselves and that of future generations selfishly,
A climate catastrophe apocalyptically,

In that this is modern man's fate there's some inevitability,
The 'culprit' being the mixed blessing of science and technology,

Which by vanquishing so imperiously,
The powerlessness presided over by the dark ages of religious hegemony,
Placed the future of each man in his own hands seemingly,
And honestly, though not to the extent advertised—obviously,
Today each man is more the captain of his own ship—verily,
But alas, perversely,
'Tis not an outcome that necessarily,
For modern man ends merrily,

For the more we know how and what a better future makes and breaks,
The more from our today it takes,
As this question our psyche grates:
'Are we doing today what a better tomorrow necessitates?',
The more anxiety it creates,

So it seems we pay for the inexorable forward march of man's progress,
With a future ordained stress,
'*The fool with all his other faults also has this...*' as Epicurus long ago did profess,
'*he is always getting ready to live*'—a case of modern regress.

Happiless

Infatuated with its chase our age,
Apparently around seven steps is all it takes so self-help is all the rage,
But heed the warning of many a great sage:
Tis akin to chasing your tail,
Faster and faster we spin but to no avail,
And worse, as we grit our teeth and flail,
We stray further and further away from our holy grail,

For that which we naysay is but a good feeling, like chocolate eating,
Which evolution for its ends of survival and procreation must make fleeting,
So that in their direction,
We must keep losing and getting an erection,
So against perpetual euphoria—our bodies and brains fight tooth and nail,
Dooming such a quest to end up an epic fail,

And, it gets worse, for the good sensation the more we pine,
The more our minds aggrandize inflating it impossibly divine,
Setting up a letdown when it's meh—not so fine,
On which we can only but put a rationalizing shine,

So don't ever think about it—easier said than done—yes, it's hard,
But you gotta start somewhere to its burden discard,
So to stop playing its game,
First stop saying its name,
Instead give yourself up to who and that which you love,

You know—where you feel like you fit like a glove,
And don't just accept but relish,
Your road's ups and downs, bumps and bruises—go so far as to cherish,
You're in love—there's nothing else to think thereof and no need to embellish,
And, what you'll get out of your labor of love is no mere fleeting good feeling,
But indeed permanent and profound purpose and meaning,

For infinitely superior to the snake oil drivel which vends the hysteria,
That man can wallow in perpetual euphoria,
But only sets us up to fail and fall into dysphoria,
Is the immeasurably more meaningful Aristotelian eudemonia,

Which together with doing what you love, as outlined above,
Holds that the 'Good Life' is one whereof:
The highest virtues man should pursue,
Become incarnated in you,

So that bludgeon, that word with its self-defeating dictates so absurd,
Never again in your head let it be heard,
Come—let's begin as of right now,
To disavow that oh so modern sacred cow.

Nocissism

Gen Z taking their zillionth selfie—up themselves so—enough to get high,
Presidents to rappers demanding them we deify,
Tweeting, making TikToks about every trivial thing we do, feel and buy,
The age of 'Me, Myself and I',
Pop Psychology's new gravy train and bad guy,

Fact: Narcissism is a real personality disorder—none can reasonably deny,
But from shrinks with on lucrative therapy and publications one eye,
To exes who their broken hearts are aching to pacify,
Tis all too expedient to cast a wider net than to which the truth will testify,
So with objectivity's sharp scalpel let's give it a try,

Now, some primp and preen like peacocks beautify,
While some do surely think themselves the moon and the sky,
Irregardless of whether their talents and feats their conceits justify,
But either nor both are sufficient to a diagnosis of narcissism qualify,

And here's why:
See the Myth of Narcissus—careful now—tends to stultify,
For what it inexorably does is over-imply,
That it was mere vanity that led our antihero awry,
Whereas, the egomaniac pure, though certainly a gadfly,
To be diagnosed a narcissist, along with other would-be elements that vie,
A dual-edged essential must satisfy,

Firstly, they must be completely unable to others anything but objectify,
The other is but a thing: if its features aren't useful or desirable, bin it bye-bye,
And, consequently, toward these 'chess pieces' on whom they rely,
For no less than their ego's sustenance, technically termed 'Narcissistic Supply',
To the suppliers' feelings not an iota of empathy can the narcissist in kind apply,

Sure, the ones a little more worldly and sly,
Can sing the odd empathetic lullaby,
But lest they mollify,
Remember—they are leeches seeking only to suck your blood dry,

So most peep's occasional selfishness and vainglory—let not belie,
For oft it's the situation or a fleeting mood that we should instead vilify,

But it's in vogue nowadays so we're prone to make superficial diagnoses on the fly,
In an irony so wry,
For we're guilty of the very same sin for which the narcissist we crucify,
When we wantonly way over-diagnose then the 'narcissism epidemic' we decry,
Where all we have is a benign nocissism scare despite all the hue and cry.

Still Nocissism

Oh how badly you want to believe if you've been a long-suffering puppet,
In this one karmic comeuppance—alas, if only 'twas true what we so covet,

The psych pros to us throw bones,
That 'neath those designer clothes in the nude their low self-esteem groans,
That narcissists sit atop fake and fragile thrones,

But, believe it or not, for most it's not mere mirrors and smoke,
The narcissist believes their own hype—no joke,
And the narcissist's superpower is an invincible cloak,
It cannot be breached and will not be broke,
For no sooner to their immaculate self-conception the slightest poke,
RED ALERT!—deny, deflect, gaslight, project—psychological defenses invoke,
'Offense is the best defense' so careful lest you provoke,
For it's the unsuspecting interlocutor's jugular that the narcissist will choke,

In terms of maintaining a positive self-image, at least, a psychic masterstroke,
And herein lies the golden nugget about which psychology hasn't spoke,
To beat reality to a positive self-image is an uphill, often impossible, slowpoke,
But self-delusion—now that comes naturally to the average broad and bloke,
Hence, narcissism can be thought of as an ego efficiency cheat 'toke',
Or akin to the ego doing lines of coke,

On 'Narcissistic Rage' you and me the empathetic dope,
May even pin our pining hearts' hope,

Their brittle shells surely must evince they're just weaklings struggling to cope,
That inside is a warm human yolk,
Just like us feeling folk,
We may even pity them, buying this psychobabble trope,
But, '*How could you!?*' and '*How dare you!!*'—ain't the same—hell nope!

Insurance Premium

'*Prevention is better than cure*' to be guided by this no harm,
So don't forget to put new batteries in your smoke alarm,
And take your flu shots as per Big Pharm,
And hydrate and apply that moisturizing balm,
And insure your belongings before your trip to Vietnam,
It's your 2nd Amendment right—so perhaps consider keeping a firearm,

With prevention who can have a qualm?

But here's the thing,
About being so 'high-functioning',
So acutely hyper plugged-in—a tightly wound spring,
To not only the 'Big T' tragedies that fate may bring:
The outrageous arrows and slings—but to every potential tincy sting and ding,

You end up your life's super: on loop box-ticking,
Then self-auditing and nitpicking,
Superintending—forgetting to live too busy finicking,

The longer your checklist,
As you work your way down, even if there's nothing you have missed,
Before you can complete it, the top is liable to again your attention insist,
And as a modern hypochondriac who are you to resist?
Here yet another reason why modern anxiety won't desist,

Believe it or not—there is such a thing as taking it on the chin,
Scraped elbows and knees? You're better off growing a thicker skin,
Tis all well and good preventative medicine,
But preventative living if not a modern mortal sin,
Then most definitely a big no-win,

So from the plethora of for-profit precautions modernity makes saleable,
Pick and choose only the most indispensable not just because it's available,
For in the currency of life there's a hefty insurance premium payable.

Privacy Issues

It goes without saying—don't steal my identity,
In my name commit not crime nor obscenity,

But privacy we've taken almost unto absurdity being so uptight about its propriety,
Rendering it yet another cause of modern anxiety,

When Google and Instagram,
Harvest my data to target ads to sell me a pram or a jar of jam,
Even that pesky spam,
Should I really give a damn?
Does all this really amount to such a scam?
A deep state-corporate overlord nefarious nexus flimflam?
When from social media, at least, I could easily be on the lam,

'There's no such thing as a free lunch',
When you clicked 'Yes, I Agree', you must have had more than a hunch,

Sure Cambridge Analytica and Facebook adulterated Brexit and the 2016 election,
But don't forget for this—definitely an egregious dereliction,
They faced punitive consequences just enough to nudge course correction,
Besides, to lay so much blame on propaganda's surgical injection,
Is to bury one's head to the electorate's uncritical predilection,
It wasn't at the point of a gun—Trump was very much their selection,

Maybe it's not privacy so much as that,
I've come to take myself too seriously being a product of this modern habitat,
I've been sold that I'm such a fat cat,
Influenced into becoming such a self-important brat,
That everything's precious about me down to even the tinciest trivial stat,
Making it hard to face the fact that Big Data correctly considers me but a sprat,

So I lash back against being treated like a 'doormat',
Taking issue with privacy 'violations', more like circumambulations, I don my high-hat,
With the indignation formerly reserved for an aristocrat.

Pro-Long

Hundreds of years of science and technology,
The very best of man's ingenuity,
Four industrial revolutions, supposedly,
All to grow this cornucopian Christmas-esque temptation tree,
Called modern industry,
Alas, only to see that so many of its fruits are forbidden for they poison me,

Every indulgence it seems doth some newfangled cancer augur,
But who cares when life expectancy is so much longer?
But that which doesn't kill me, apparently, hasn't made me stronger,
I'm a coward that dies many times for modernity also a deft fear-monger,

For in selling prevention and cure,
Just as much as in selling that which necessitates them—the lure,
There's as much if not more profit for sure!
Which in turn gives rise to the alarmist entrepreneur,

Cruel and unusual so,
Definitely a First World problem though,
How as the goodies in the proverbial candy store grow and grow,
More and more I've got to fight myself and resist '*NO! NO!*',

So I'm floundering here far, far from distant death,
Not dreaming up ways of expanding life's richness and breadth,
But unnecessarily rendered a hypochondriac wretch,
Battling as if already gasping for my last breath down my final stretch,

Maybe when he dismissed thus some things Epicurus conveniently forgot—
'*Where I am death is not, and where death is I am not*',
For tis an inescapable corollary of human consciousness—deny this one cannot,
To think about and fear its own annihilation, hopefully just not a lot,
So modern man—easy there!—on death's trail you're way, way too hot,
So much so that you're at risk of losing life's plot!

Sometimes I wonder if at Shady Oaks as my body inevitably decays,
Wistful through a dementia haze,
I'll reminisce my 'salad days',
And if as I bid '*So, so, so long*'—I'll reappraise,
For quantity so oft quality betrays,
Regretting that more than living my years all I did was prolong them lengthways.

Blues Clues

If you're forever blue, there ain't nothing wrong with you,
'Cause depression just ain't true,

Now I don't mean that your neuro-chemical stew,
Is maybe not askew,
And hey, I'm not glibly asking you—'*Why so glum?*',
When you're down in the dumps, chum,
Nor telling you to '*Just snap out of it*'—to your pain I'm not numb,

But what I am doing is, to the medical establishment contrarily,
Positing that the melancholy verily,
Not of all but of the majority vast,
Is actually the natural reaction of the healthy, and thusly should be recast,

Just the same way your hand doth instinctively retreat,
From a fire's harmful heat,
Sometimes pain and unease,
Are not about symptoms and disease,
To the subject are not internal these,
Instead their maladies,
Are an external signal to up and leave hence to progress they're the keys,

So before you self-medicate,
Or fill in that prescription to sedate,
Or a couch prelate teaches you tricks and techniques to grin and tolerate,

Listen—you wretch on the edge,
Else your only way out may be off a ledge,

Take a closer look at the structures and strictures of society,
Ask what caused so many fish so suddenly to become so sickly?
Perhaps it's the fish-tank water's toxicity,
Thus removing the fish and treating them individually,
Then replacing them is an exercise in futility,
Therefore necessitating, imperatively,
An 'Out with the old; in with the new' re-think radically,

So if the wall—sociocultural-political-economic,
In which you're just another brick,
If that which passes as sane,
Is what is indeed deranged and therefore your real bane,
Look only in the mirror and not out the window pane,
And it is you that'll appear insane,

Because it doth falsely point the finger and accuse,
Ourselves of this atomized pathologization we must disabuse,
Though to tell them they're even in water doth fish famously bemuse,
Nevertheless, for the causes of the modern blues,
Squarely to the superstructure we must look for clues.

Powers Be

Is this all a conspiracy orchestrated diabolically by the powers-that-be?
Not just victory and tragedy like the Moon Landing and the WTC,
But a Matrix-style warping of the very fabric of our reality,

Think for a moment if this were all run by an evil secret society,
Some such cabal like the Illuminati,
How different would our day-to-day be in kind and degree?

Despite mind-boggling advances in technology,
Would we be working longer and harder—never taking it easy,
All to buy things we're taught to want but don't need really?

And lest in our little respite we question,
They'd design devices to commandeer away our attention,
À la Brave New World—a sedating, albeit, digital concoction,
To drug us with distraction,

To philosophers and artists we'd pay no heed,
For much thought and time taketh to sprout their mind-seed,
Indeed, we'd feel we have no need,
For the elite would spoon-feed,
With 'fake news', Facebook memes, Insta reels and celebrity tweets to mislead,
So we'd worship a creed,
Which to our detriment will only serve their greed,

And when the rat-race has made you a head case,
Your doctor on 'the take' won't hesitate to crawl into your headspace,
Prescribe Prozac, Xanax, Ritalin et al so you'll be in Big Pharma's ironclad embrace,

Now, some of you must be concurring that this is spot on and nodding along,
With others disagreeing, just as strong,
But both are wrong,

See all of this is true—
Just look around you,
But little if any,
Is imposed upon many,

'Bad Faith' the philosopher Sartre called this fake,
He insisted you do have freedom—any path you can take,
Any choice you can make,
But afraid of the consequences' weight,
You deny your freedom and call it fate,
Pointing a lame finger of blame, your innate human agency you abdicate,

To think 'they' have our well-being at heart—agreed—smacks of rank naivety,
But to believe this is all a meticulous master plan executed to a tee,
George Soros, Hillary and Dr. Fauci,
Sat hooded at a round table lit spookily,
Conniving to perpetuate the hegemony of Free Masonry,
By plotting to spread Corona using 5G!
Is the kind of bunkum and baloney believed for the expediency of the psyche,
It is merely psychological escapist artistry,

In fact, if at all, it's forces not people that oppress me,
Indeed, that I've been blindfolded, that I do not see,
The real powers-that-be: capitalism, culture and history,
Such that I let them off scot-free,
Now that is the biggest conspiracy!

Judge Mental

'No Judgment' that modern refrain,
Is as pernicious as it is inane,

Not on bias nor whim nor fancy,
But grounded on human nature's exigency,
Upon which, at this stage of our story, we all should be able to agree,
We ought to parse right from wrong and then decree,
Not spinelessly agree to disagree,
Or, far worse, give license to the cultural relativist to rampage free,
To anti-intellectually spew sophistry,
And rationalize barbarity,

If we do not stand up and judge, we must accept our moral complicity,
In every egregious inhumanity,

Female genital mutilation, infanticide, 'honor' homicide,
Are we to sit on the fence and take no side?
Widows hurling themselves on funeral pyres, little girls given to old men as child brides,
Are we to deny them feminism's gallant strides?
Casteism: by 'fault' of birth being ostracized,
Are we to equivocate calling this 'different' but yet still civilized?

No matter even if the oppressed,
Oblige willingly to privation—insisting it's for their own best,
We mustn't disingenuously take this to attest,

That tis so, ipso facto—we must contest,
Because the child's cognition hasn't sufficiently progressed,
And the adult's has been by culture possessed,

Cultural or otherwise, the relativist's dogmatic disposition,
Of leaving each to his own free of any inquisition,
Let alone any opposition,
Is radically antithetical to progress's ambition,
For if everything is to be left as it is without imposition,
Then we'd better hope against hope that the way things are and all tradition,
Are the best they can be for thence there can be no further expedition,

I shudder to think of our fate,
If those who came before us this duty did not effectuate,
History stillborn before she could fully gestate,
Or stopped in her tracks just to sentimentality placate,
We mightn't even be here to have this debate,
If the duel of ideals we never did tolerate,

What makes this abrogation all the more of a shame,
Is that though of the inviolability of diversity they talk a big game,
Tis mostly a masquerade—tis not the real aim,
Unmasked tis but a melodramatic over-correction ever so lame,
To soothe the festering guilt of former oppressors who've internalized the blame,
A mea culpa with a florid dance and a grandiloquent name,

A case of the modern conscience to seek equilibrium getting sentimental,
In the process to progress being detrimental,
A case of modernity getting it wrong monumental,
Going judge mental.

Perfetishism

Perfect parenting, straight-A grades, pink of health, not a wrinkle of age,
A meticulous masterplan made for each life stage,
Focus never wanders, not a minute of wastage,
Even down to immaculately disposing of the garbage,

It strikes into the modern soul terror,
Committing even the teensiest error,
Ah! If only we could outlaw every last flaw,
Surely that would be the missing piece in the 'happiness' jigsaw,

Groan not—it's not to rehash that 'No one is perfect' cliché I endeavor,
But rather to the very notion of error from perfection sever,

What if perfection was living life large,
Blunders, disasters, warts and all—think Homer versus Marge,
Into life's glorious uncertainties a headlong charge,

The perfectionist then would not be the obsessive-compulsive hair-splitter,
But the don't-sweat-the-small-stuff home-run hitter,

Who will be unafraid to from the linear to the lateral digress,
Who actually hopes that fate with bumps and detours will bless,
Who will count a goal achieved imperfectly nevertheless as progress,
Thus declare the mission a magnificent success,

What I effervesce of—this vivacious incarnation,
Looks up to the Titan-Olympian god ideal with aspiration,
Impassioned by libidinal intoxication,
Living—a work of art—therefore no one flawless formulation,
At its transcendent pinnacle—a Promethean creation,

Meaning over mistake,
Heroism over headache,
Forgiveness over flagellation,
Humor over humiliation,
Novelty over neuroticism,
Possibility over pedantism,
Master morality over slave servility,
Viva virility over cuckolded conformability,

May a Renaissance Übermensch perfectionism,
Dethrone modernity's penny wise-pound foolish perfetishism.

Mind-Squandering

Many a modern proponent,
Espouses one to 'Stay in the moment',
Veer not—of single-minded focus become a masterful exponent,
For mind-wandering they insist is well-being's opponent,

Mid-coitus drifting off to what's next,
Or at a candle-lit dinner sending a text,
Or even worse texting during sex—perhaps the worst kind of sext!
Is all too easy to rile against self-righteousness flexed,

Tis but a straw man—at trending psycho-babble's behest,
Mind-wandering assessed at its worst—not its best,

For what of the flights of fancy that flit,
Shooting the breeze—the here-and-now they don't quite fit,
Yet that luck would have it on a fortuitous flower chance to sit,
Cross-pollination—EUREKA!—a new sweet spot hit!

Daydream free-bird oh ironic isn't it,
Rolling their eyes at thee who's always dreary reality sunlit,
In an age where creativity is held up as holy writ,
That he who doth so posit,
Is an unwitting hypocrite,
Who by simultaneously persuading you to mind-wandering quit,
Cocksure that tis tantamount to mind-squandering, though the opposite,
In the same breath your creative wings doth slit.

Onlyness

I'm lonely—but why?
In my loneliness as I writhe, I wrestle—to solve this I try, I try,

Modern life so fast, I'm always busy,
Between work, workouts, chores and errands which spin me dizzy,
I can't even spare a jiffy,

Extended family a thing of the past—wah-wah,
And the nuclear family doesn't look like it'll last—blah-blah...

But there's more to my desolate plight,
Than this 'busyness' and 'family' trope so trite,

In days gone by when loneliness didn't so blight,
We weren't such pedants, so uptight,

Basically all we needed was a chummy warm body to pass the time,
But now we won't settle for company any less than our reflection mime:
Who with our every word and thought doesn't rhyme,
Who doesn't perfectly fit our personal-political paradigm,

Our personalities must vibe,
Shared interests we must together imbibe,
To my values you must subscribe,
Rage retweet my online diatribe,

Cancel whom I proscribe,
Republican or Democrat—we must be of the same tribe,

Even the slightest deviance disqualifies for me the relationship purist,
Far from the N-word, even a whiff of stumbling right-wing is racist,
And if I'm a QAnon conspiracy theorist,
I can't bear the sight of my woke antagonist,

Human connection I've winnowed thereby I've narrowed the field so,
And, my tribe? Beloved is my bubble-mate sis and bro,
But they're not always around though,
They're mostly online—ones and zeros—somewhat faux:
A face-to-face, press-the-flesh—no show,

If only I could let a few more things go,
I could crawl out of modern individualism's solo silo,
But I'm no traitor, I'm true to the cause nouveau:
'Be myself even in spite of myself'—so hell no!

My loneliness stemming from my rigidity on exclusivity and purity,
Finicky, persnickety,
My 'ONLY'ness keeps me in solitary confinement captivity.

Friendtertainer

Friendship one of life's most precious gifts indeed,
So much in common or so in sync each an open book for the other to read,
Someone who just 'gets you'—explaining yourself no need,
Who's happy for you when you succeed,
Who's there for you in word and deed,
Who for you is ready to bleed,
All of this I readily concede,

But besides all these hosannas high-flown,
A friend is a source of something more down-home which the smartphone,
Insidiously flatters to clone,

See just their presence—just chilling,
Shooting the breeze and tea spilling,
Was more than just time killing,
'Twas an entertainment fulfilling,
Which kept the relationship's wheels spinning being quite thrilling,

But modern life tempts with candies saccharine sweet,
That are also irresistibly easier to eat,
As a characteristically clinical economist might drumbeat,
Its greater 'transaction costs' alone means with its modern rivals it cannot compete,
Thus rendering friendship as entertainment obsolete,

Why not on your couch lay,
For just a few taps and clicks away,
Are all your fav shows, food and the games you wanna play?
Whereas—weekend plans?
You gotta wear pants—unlike Only Fans,

So as it becomes ever easier to binge,
On friendship doth this ever more impinge,
Less and less time with my friends do I spend,
For to do so seems like a lot of energy to expend,
Thence between us a continental drift inexorably does extend,

And now this entertainment-convenience calculus has drifted us so apart,
That all the deeper refuges and greater glories of friendship—its beating heart,
I am deprived of for in my friend's life I play but a bit part,

Now in hindsight it seems like a no-brainer:
It was when I gave you up as an entertainer,
My friendtertainer—my sister, my brother from another mother,
I made you but a distant other.

Socialies

Though some extroverted whilst some more demure,
Man is a social animal—for sure,
But this obvious truth another subtler one doth easily obscure,

To be with others is as natural as breathing,
But how this comes about is not without a convoluted process of teething,

Hunting and gathering in groups,
In the trenches with the troops,
Many cooks were needed to make soups,

It took a village—parenting splitting,
We always needed to be close whether farming or fishing—fighting for survival teeth-gritting,
And 'twas as a spin-off from wresting a living to baby-sitting,
That one with another ended up clicking—'twas quite unwitting,

But thanks to mass produced alienation from the likes of Ford,
The convenience modern gadgets afford,
Amazon delivering to our doorsteps everything down to groceries—a smorgasbord,
And now with remote work becoming the norm across-the-board,
Survival and production necessitate not as many of the social bonds of old,
But alas! That just means to fraternize now we must call in from the cold,

It turns out that man was only a natural so bold,
Where the ice was broken for him when by the task he was brought into the fold,

And kept there long enough until was crossed a min 'get to know' threshold,
The ubiquity of the school friend and the coworker romance—in the same mold,
Ask yourself—what in common do they hold?

To grab your phone,
Message or—ick!—hear that ringtone,
Occasioned by no work nor necessity but sociability's own,
The rare social butterfly letting alone,
I can hear the shy caterpillars groan,

Of the most social species—ironic I realize,
But when the next loved one of loneliness dies,
Tragic yet no surprise,
For '*Come out of your shell*', '*Get out of your comfort zone*' we may aphorize,
But tis naïve to expect and advise—
'*Come on! Just up and socialize!*',
Tis but a bunch of social lies.

Family Freud

Grandpa's body only found by its stench,
Once a year around a turkey we sit and clench,
Hoping that Uncle Earl into the small-talk détente won't throw a racist wrench,

No grandma the torn and broken to sew and mend,
No idle porch chitchat to long summer days end,
No cousin nor aunt more than a Facebook friend,

Mom's working two jobs to just make ends meet,
Hope her new boyfriend, like the last, won't cheat,
Still better than dad—I hate that fucking deadbeat,

The extended family's fate,
Which if already hasn't befallen it—a matter of debate,
Then, definitely, for the nuclear family lies in wait,

A diametrically different economy and technology,
The Feminist Movement and individualism, posits sociology,
All true—but what say you psychology?

See it's all about libidinal energy,
That magma ever simmering in each psyche volcanically,
With which modern culture has a topsy-turvy relationship of ambivalency,

Mixed messaging galore,
With one side of modernity's mouth our life-giving eros it seems to deplore,
Far, far before oedipal and electra urges we even dare to explore,
With a near Victorian ardor of yore,
From what sweetmeat decadent treat not to buy at the grocery store,
To not asking out that sexy coworker we got the hots for,
A neo-puritanical self-denial modern culture doth implore,

Of many an age and even today in the pre-modern Third World tis true—nothing new,
That culture doth self-indulgence eschew,

But then in a Jekyll & Hyde about-face,
Of hedonism an all-consuming embrace,
From cheeseburger stuffed crust pizza,
To 24/7 porn on-demand and juicy gossip on your fav diva,
Just do it—and put it on your Visa,

But as modern life with its lure of thousands of tiny little orgasms goad,
You into blowing your libidinal load,
This wanton masturbatory depletion does not for the family well bode,

Now, now this is not about copulation per se,
Not in a physically incestuous way,
But if you want to keep the familial circulatory system from gray decay,
Firstly, conserve your libidinal energy—do not let it cum or go astray,
Then though its veins and arteries under the skin of day-to-day may lay,
Unceasingly pump through them the hot red lifeblood of eros each and every day,

Then you may well find the remedy for that evermore hollow modern family void,
Is a reinjection of family Freud.

House-Hunted

What's behind,
The minimalist's peace of mind?
To merely the freedom from the overwhelm of clutter it's not confined,
Indeed, decluttering is more so a means designed,
To eventually win a far more valuable freedom—freedom from the grind,

For copious consumption needless to say,
With more hours of slog most have to pay,
As the saying doth convey:
'*We buy things we don't need with money we don't have...*', and it's no cliché,
'Tis, indeed, the espoused modern way,
So as to keep the wheels of consumer capitalism spinning away,

Ah, if it only were that easy for the minimalist no matter how true-blue,
To jump off the hamster wheel and the rat-race eschew!
For you see the minimalist will be trapped so long as he's in the few,
And the unbreakable padlock on his rat cage will be the housing issue,

Like many things it boils down to economics 101,
It's supply-and-demand that makes the minimalist's laid-back plans come undone,

Compare the minimalist to he who is not,
It stands to reason the slogger's income will be greater by a lot,
And if they are in the majority, high prices seem like the predictable upshot,
For a lot of loaded buyers in a bidding war is for sellers the jackpot,

Unless, it's a product where it's easy to up supply,
Where the faucet could be opened, easy as pie,
And whoosh—out the product would fly,
Now thanks to modern technology and logistics to many products this does apply,
Made in China or Chennai to labor standards turning a blind eye,
On a ship and in a jiffy on Amazon Prime ready to buy,
Housing, however, does not so readily comply,

To simplify and elucidate,
Consider the minimalist's fate,
If all that was up for grabs in terms of real estate,
Were a hundred apartments in one building for our enlightened cheapskate,
And he had to bid against hordes of sloggers grinding every day till late,
With incomes to their hustle commensurate or which at least strongly correlate,
Since even the hardcore minimalist who other wants may abnegate and moderate,
The need for a roof over their head can't obviate,
This in turn will necessitate,
That the would-be minimalist reluctantly has to the infernal grind capitulate,
And if healthcare and college are not at the very least subsidized by the state,
For definitely healthcare—there's no debate,
And nowadays college too are needs which one can't eliminate,
Nor find substitutes for so as to circumnavigate,
And like housing both their supply are not amenable to with a 'push of a button' escalate,
So piling on his back on top of the burdensome housing weight,
The minimalist's predicament this only doth exacerbate,

So, alas, minimalism is priced-out when with these market realities it's confronted,
By healthcare and college it may be shunted,
Either way, at every turn in the cross-hairs of the real estate market minimalism is house-hunted.

Sharing Economy

Lest you're hard-pressed,
May I suggest,
Work a little less, live a little more and be less stressed,
By sharing your job with the rest,

Though the Confucian and Protestant Ethic for whom work is the duty prime,
Will malign for tis blasphemy to its paradigm,
Everyone working 'part-time' ain't no crime,
In fact, Keynes predicted by 2030—so high-time!
The work week will be 15 hours—work-life balance sublime!

I know, I know it's a sea-change to digest,
And—'*That's not in my best-interest!*'—I hear your dismissive protest,
But maybe one day it'll be you that the 'Invisible Hand' will divest,

For automation has long since the demand for factory jobs depressed,
As the Opioid Crisis and blue collar workers will attest,
And the election of Trump expressed,
And soon AI that fast-learning foe, that mutant of human-machine incest,
Will leave white collar workers too dispossessed,

Perhaps only when in the new economy you feel like an unwelcome welfare pest,
And the rampaging ranks of the 'rest' foment social unrest,
With your hands outstretched to the blessed,
You might find yourself bleating this very same behest:
That for you and the greatest good—a sharing economy is best.

Maximalist Comrade

Oh for sure 'Less is more' so I'd love to go if not totz boho,
Then most certainly Marie Kondo,
But even though for the simple life I'm all gung-ho,
Not to mention that it'll save me a load of dough,
It's not just all about me, you know,

Look—I need nor want that brand spanking new car nor Prada,
But I can't selfishly up and renounce '*I'm satisfied—no more—nada!*',
Come on—consider the bigger picture, the whole enchilada,

Just think of the millions of jobs,
Miserly minimalism robs!

Think of the moms and dads who wouldn't be able,
To put food on the table,
All downhill from here given a house of cards economy already teetering unstable,
Soon the state Medicare, Medicaid, Social Security and the military to afford unable,
Sans my charitable consumerism things will descend into a dystopian fable,

So despite myself I crawl to the mall,
Altruistically on Amazon gather a huge haul,
Second mortgage, thumping car loans, maxed credit cards and all,
Just doing my part as a citisumer ever so small,
So that economic armageddon on my brothers and sisters will not befall!

Drag Nett

Something so simple we forget,
To assess in terms of nett:
That from whatever we ultimately get—
What we give we must offset,
For instance, sure I'd like to have that Corvette,
But only if less the sweat plus the debt,
I'm happier than I was at the outset,

So why do we suffer such paralysis,
In this simple cost benefit analysis?
The answer's even simpler—given human avarice:
For tis only on the 'benefits' side marketing places all the emphasis,

And whether religious, political or corporate none can reasonably insist,
That propaganda doesn't get ever more sophisticated and harder to resist,

So ISIS and MAGA are just as adept,
As Silicon Valley and the corporate jet set,
At using psychology and technology and beaming through the Internet,
Leading you on to believe that it's most definitely your best bet,
To scuffle for deals on Black Friday and, till not so long ago, smoke that cigarette,
To drive German, wear Italian and sip French like a marketer's marionette,
To blow yourself up for 72 virgins' silhouette,
To storm the Capitol steps spearheaded by a vet,
To save 'Murica from the DEMonic child eating threat,

And if we are beset,
By 'Buyer's Regret',
There's always that trusty accomplice to the propagandists aide and abet,
'*I'm so stupid as to be duped by a bad bargain*' our self-concept doth upset,
Cognitive dissonance it doth beget,
So instead the gains we pad to mollify away our fret,

But neither this 'after-sales self-service' known as 'Post-Purchase Rationalization',
Nor any other such cognitive consolation,
Can lead to the mitigation,
Of the real costs and consequences in any tangible substantiation,
So the buyer is left to pay if not the ultimate price of self-annihilation,
Then at least with workaholism to debt to incarceration,
And, good luck looking to the seller for salvation!

In all this the ironic joke:
Modern man who fancies himself educated and emancipated—not under any yoke,
Unlike his predecessors Dark Age and Medieval folk,
At gain - loss is still a bit of a mental slowpoke,
So more often than worldliness would warrant ends up dead, in jail or broke,
Or unnecessarily stressed at risk of heart attack or stroke,
In other words—to the dragnett of bad bargains modern man still ain't woke.

Progressive Entrepreneur

They tell me life is a battle, a struggle—it's supposed to be hard,
For wanting it easy, I'm a moocher, a loser—irredeemable not avant-garde,

But they haven't stopped to ponder—if the work week keeps getting ever long,
Sleep forgone,
Anxiety every morn,
Stress the unremovable thorn,
The hapless worker forlorn,
Whom by cancer and clogged arteries plagued and worn,
Mother Nature pillaged with scorn,
Leaving armageddon for the unborn,
Is it me that just doesn't belong?
Or is it civilization that's in the wrong direction gone?

In 1760, at future's dawn, the promise was this:
Slave 16 hours a day in a soul-crushing mind-numbing industrial abyss,
So that for your children robots and androids would soon usher in apotheosis,

For where drudgery we abolish,
Thereby the soul we nourish,
Therein my god-like human potential will flourish,
It is this, not sloth, for which I wish,

And, given the stage of technological advancement we are now at which,
Tis reasonable to expect and demand to be both free and rich,

So name-call me 'lazy' all you want—such a vacuous modern slur,
Only I'm not; I'm just forward-thinking I'd aver,

Besides, not with toil and strife,
But with spontaneity to beauty, curiosity to creativity—the finest pursuits in life,
I'm ever busy—my mind with them rife,

So how about you consider this to my imagination bender, my daydream adventure,
An IPO to come invest in my venture,

And when you make it big—when you become a life connoisseur,
Then, on me, the title I hope you confer:
Progressive entrepreneur.

BiFamiliarity

On Amazon billions of thingamajigs, millions of shows on Netflix,
Yet starved for choice when it comes to politics,

Ironic, then, that it's thought a bane of modern life,
That tis with choice too rife,

Endless varieties of trinkets and trivialities we consider our birthright,
Yet with riding a donkey or an elephant so tiresome and trite,
To exercise our inalienable rights—somehow with this plight,
We were pathetically alright,

You'd think as born-and-bred citisumers of consumer society,
As we do of our free market economy with a gluttonous insatiety,
Of our hard-won democracy we'd have demanded more representative variety,

Right to Left, Left to Right, hither and thither, this way and that,
Shuffling teensy-weensy then waffling back with the guile of a diplomat,
All the while essentially standing pat,
It's been basically the same old hat:
Tory or Labour, Republican or Democrat,

I mean really how can it be a capacious political spectrum,
When dominated by the duopolistic two-party system?

In ancient Greece, how apt to mention,
That an idiot was he who to the politics of his city-state paid no attention,
For it was the modern apprehension,
And indeed oft the reprehension,
To politics which devolved into a dire lack of comprehension,

Apathetically only every four years or so,
Even then voter turnout low,
Not caring enough and/or able to weigh con and pro,
Of a political manifesto,
Whether voting how people like us always have or swinging to and fro,
Or going with our gut or eeny-meeny-miny-moe,
Or picking the 'lesser of two evils'—we went with the flow,
We never even considered giving the 'no-hoper' a go,
In a self-fulfilling prophecy we were complicit, obliviously though:
'*Why waste a vote on a poor schmo,*
Who's got no chance? Hell no!',
But when everyone thinks so, the 'no hoper' really has no chance, ipso facto,

They may say that familiarity breeds contempt,
But the known devils over the unknown angels did tempt,
So even though the establishment we detested,
We simultaneously always re-elected,

Even those of us who fancy ourselves idealistic,
Turned out to be unwitting pawns of realpolitik so machiavellian and slick,
For when it came to genuine alternatives,
We were all de facto hawkish conservatives,

This inevitably served only to embolden and ossify the regime,
Until our simmering discontent boiled into a raging head of steam,
Which drove us to take a perilous plunge extreme,

Thus in politics the great lament:
Bifamiliarity breeds establishment,
Until, that is, in the form of Trump it meant,
Of the Union and democracy itself a cataclysmic dismemberment.

Politically Inept

Tis painfully plain to see that Right from Left has never been so polarized,
Perhaps this is the politics of the past romanticized,
But it used to be mainly ideological differences which opposition catalyzed,
Yet when the greater good demanded it as one we did rise,
Our differences we were able to compartmentalize,
But now we so otherize then soon demonize,
That to prophesize we are heading for another civil war is not to catastrophize,

It sounds fair and balanced to safely sanitize,
That 'Both sides are in the wrong', but to do so is to falsely equalize,
Which side climate change denies,
Believes 9/11 to Sandy Hook to be all staged lies,
Fears that biological men in women's sports will their daughters brutalize,
Pedals that chemicals in the water will frogs homosexualize,
Scaremongers that Jewish space lasers will zap you from the skies,
Prescribes bleach and horse tranquilizer to immunize whilst vaccines villainize,
Gerrymanders so as to minorities disenfranchise,
Race-baits that the Illuminati with migration diabolically devise,
To replace the White race and cause America's demise,
Plots to elections deny and delegitimize,
Foments a violent insurrection to the Capitol terrorize?

Is it the Democrats those baby eating pedophiles,
Who supposedly all that America stands for reviles?

No, this conspiracy and fascist shite,
Is exclusively from the Right,

Political Advisory: from here on in,
May cause snowflakes more than a little chagrin,

Information bubbles,
Lack of social media muzzles,
Exacerbated by demagogues who fact and fiction machiavellianly muddle,
True—all of these, indeed, pieces of the mis/disinformation puzzle,

But here's the 'Elephant' in the newsroom,
Which we sweep under the rug with a politically-correct broom:
Conservatives are not as smart as liberals—boom!

Though, disconfirming facts have always been convenient to ignore,
Be honest—we are not living in Orwell's 1984,
There's a wealth of sound sources—just click or tap to explore,
Which can disabuse you of the absurd and dangerous mal-ideas—before!
They break in through your mind's backdoor,
So, to be fair, Fox News to Info Wars as much as liberals rightly abhor,
Are not solely to blame for the culture war,
For sorely lacking critical thinking acumen is at the rot's core,

Certainly education, especially primary, we need to focus on much more,
But the real villain is the zeitgeist which renders sophisticated ideas a bore,
That is baffled by any learning for its own sake for it seems like a profitless chore,

It is the glorification of anti-intellectualism which could mean we're done for,
This is how the West was lost—we will lament unless against it we implore,

But the libtards about political incorrectness gets so sore,
Label them elitist their tails timorously tuck between their legs—so therefore:
The politically inept are left more and more to the Trumps of the world adore.

Liberalschism

The Enlightenment ideal of free speech dies in irony,
Strangled on the campus of the university,
Under this newfangled 'liberal bias'— this politically correct tyranny,
The homophobe and the white supremacist,
The Islamophobe and the male chauvinist,
The woke police take pride in having vanquished and free speech having abolished,
And why should we be astonished?
For liberalism was never in the masses' wheelhouse, you see,
It was never their cup of tea,

The philosopher's mind—liberalism's womb,
It was they whom,
Braving the buffoon and the goon even the threat of the early tomb,
Raised and reared her in their doting intellectual cocoon,
Before she could butterfly out on revolutionary winds when history opportune,
To confront the inhumane zeitgeist at high noon,

And like the attentive parent best knows their child,
While most others by what's merely on the outside are beguiled,
Sans the philosopher's cerebral guile,
What the woke folks cannot or do not seem to see as they revile,
Is that 'liberal' used to be the mental stance required,
For the intellectual to do the work to which he aspired,
The open-mind which was sine qua non for the professional thinker,
If he desired with any coherent success to with the tried-and-tested tinker,

And who in doing so, more often than no,
Would expose the absurdities and depravities of the status quo,

So, in other words, liberalism also meant a capacious cognitive disposition,
But woah! Now, somehow—what an inverted position!
Liberalism comes complete—tis replete with its own dogmas and mission,

But 'A little learning is a dangerous thing',
Then, no surprise should it bring,
When mass education toward censorship egalitarianism doth sling,

For it imbues opinions and 'thoughts' still very much lay,
With an unwarranted confidence belying their naiveté,
This hubris then makes them bray,
And for the blood of free speech bay,
Though on the intellectual scale they barely weigh,

So what has come to pass: a cancer in liberalism,
A crotchety troll arisen—a liberalschism.

Hopeocracy

When the butcher and the baker,
Rise up against the dictator,
It heartens the would-be constitution maker,
Into thinking that democracy to man's very nature doth cater,
So hankering after it he will forever be an agitator or at least an appreciator,

Sorry to be a hater but this fairytale notion I must expunge,
For the masses recurrently pied-pipered by demagoguery heart-first lunge,
With a strongman from Hitler to Trump take the perilous plunge,
When, most usually, in an economic crunch,
They deliver to supposedly 'sacrosanct' democracy a gut-punch,

Only to when, 'surprise-surprise' predictably,
The oxygen of freedom is asphyxiated by tyranny,
Remonstrate and demonstrate that all they ever wanted was democracy,

Again and again this historical circularity,
Plays out for the masses expect then soon demand grand things from the polity:
Escape from poverty to ever proliferating prosperity,
Of course draining the swamp of corruption and criminality,
The security of national sovereignty,
Unfortunately, xenophobically, oft a majoritarian ethno-racial purity,
A renaissance of religiosity, civility, art, science and technology,
A return to a mythic golden age hybridized harmoniously,
With a flourishing futuristic fantasy,

Oblivious to the fact that first and foremostly,
Far from ushering in a utopia preternaturally,
Democracy's purpose is to spare them from the worst excesses of autocracy,
So, alas, they fatigue of even the most satisfactory democratic incumbency,

Disappointedly divorcing their boring old lady or potbelly for someone more sexy,
But when the honeymoon wears out all too swiftly,
They find the grass is meaner on the dictator's side—but tis too late tragically,
They've been baited-and-switched catastrophically,
By their own hopeocracy.

UnSelfie

Only our most poignant moments we used to consecrate with pics,
For a film roll only had 36 clicks,

Then to develop them we'd beeline straight,
And eagerly we'd await,
Hoping that each would just perfectly incubate,
Come out clear and bright—our big moments vividly encapsulate,
On holidays and birthdays to reminisce we'd congregate,
On the sofa huddled around albums our cherished memories we'd commemorate,

But now that pics are free,
And storage is aplenty,
Gee! We take way, way too many! Most would agree,
This alone is enough to debase the photograph into a modern banality,
But it gets worse, you see,

Social media has incentivized,
And even monetized,
Staging our pics for mass taste generalized,

That we used to just say 'Cheese' seems quaint in retrospect,
Now with the centerfold photographer's eye our pics we direct,
Only the best of the best featuring our 'best side' we select,
We edit away flaws and filter till we are Photoshop perfect,
Then, using the publicist's playbook, we project for maximum reach and effect,
Remember, the point is no longer for the picture to our moments vivisect,

Beneath the disappointment for a vast majority who find on so commercializing,
That the views, likes and cents are not materializing,
There's a far greater loss—this entire modern project is depersonalizing,

My pictures used to be,
Portraits for my autobiography—meant to be read and re-read by me,

But now they are at most quasi-autobiography laced with fiction and fantasy,
Which as I script and stage them keep me from relishing reality,
Leaving me with nothing with which to reminisce fondly,
For they happened just as much as reality TV,

What does it profit a man in actuality,
If for a tuppence of likes from social unreality,
He profanes his autobiography by performing a memory just to take an unselfie?

Status Update

All it takes is one peek at their social media highlight stream,
To glean that my friends, alas, are still so dead-set it does seem,
On climbing a ladder of absurd dimensions extreme:
Stultifyingly narrow whilst to the clouds tall supreme,
From Benzes and Beemers begin the rungs of esteem,
To villas and yachts they're lured to dream,

But before the obvious retort you shout,
Tis most natural, as if there were any doubt:
The human animal's drive to one-up each other, and on top come out,
Of this there's no two words about,

Yes, for the fittest to survive,
And then to thrive,
In the societal pecking order they must rise—for status they must strive,

For as the name itself indicates,
It's those at the top who eat first and most and get the best mates,

So that Rolex ain't about time,
Nor about that 'fine' wine anything especially sublime,
Nah, it's you versus me—it's best understood via a competitive paradigm,

But here's where capitalism turns status on its head,
You see in feudalism it was your status that decided your daily bread,

Which in turn purely by birth could be bred,
So slaves and serfs were abjectly poor and underfed,
Whereas, the lords and ladies were rich and overfed,
At least then though it was nearly impossible it must be said,
To climb the social ladder and get ahead,
If miraculously you managed to, then you'd commensurately be better fed,

But now, expensive things if you can already easily afford to buy,
You've already got what only status used to be able to supply,
You're rich! You've won! Jackpot! Bull's-eye!
Still, if it's but a drop in the ocean, conspicuous consumption I can't deny,
Can be money well-spent to turn heads and momentarily catch the eye,

But stretching every penny you don't have to buy that sports car,
With change earned from a tip jar,
Not sorry to burst your bubble—but showing-off nah,
Ain't gonna give you the lifestyle of a rock star,
Displaying that you're rich is only gonna make you poorer than you are,

But fear not if money is unforthcoming and always tight,
And buying status symbols you can't afford only worsens your plight,
This doesn't have to mean you're out of the fight,
There is another and better way to grow your 'social height',

Rather than killing yourself and planet Earth,
Only to end up feeling empty and broke in a materialism induced dearth,
The more enlightened means of substance and girth,
To settle our relative worth,
Is to follow the calling of art and beauty and games and even mirth,

Lucky are those upon whom the muses call,
Who are led by their siren song with no thought of competition at all,
For they radiate a magnetism without even trying to enthrall,
Which yet holds those in their orbit in thrall,

Now granted if it's not true passion but merely a means to an end,
There may be no social seduction dividend,
So 'Follow your passion' all the more reason to recommend,
And even if by doing so one's status does not ascend,
The pursuit itself will the meaninglessness of existence help transcend,
Therefore, than its superficial alternative in it there's much more to commend,

Certainly more so than where we congeal our transcendent zeal,
By partaking of Michelin star meals just to make Instagram reels,
And re-post and re-tweet hollow social justice appeals,
Whilst sipping exorbitant coffee beans in effete Alexander McQueen jeans,

Materialism is not at all what it has cracked up to have been,
So from it ourselves we must wean,
In a way that both keeps Mother Nature pristine,
And our species-being does not demean,
We must endeavor to be heard and seen,

It not being our conscious aim we should implicitly compete to pass on our genes,
By fulfilling and wholesome means,
And, to do so would require a status update for the philistines.

Sleep Waking

Time was when life was hard so sleep came easy,
For aching limbs and growling tummies 'twas a reprieve and relief so breezy,
Catching Zzzzzz before your head hit the floor—'twas that lemon squeezy,

Au naturel—now this seems like a reverie,
We've cast an ensemble from blue screens to caffeine as the enemy,
We need forest sounds and memory foam to 'fall' asleep with urgency,
Chamomile tea, NyQuil and Ambien—an entire pharmacy,

But the body works oppositely to the mind,
When exhausted to rest it is inclined,
Lullabying the brain in tow behind,
Whereas, for the mind stimulation and grind,
Cause it to in ever procreating thought spirals wind,
And not necessarily in the creative Newton and the apple daydreaming kind,
No, the executive function once primed,
More and more worry and vexation doth it make if it can't find,

We toss-and-turn—most not out of dread of not winning our daily bread,
Mercifully, survival, at least, required only one path of worry to tread,
No, ours is a multifarious stress: from trying to stay and get ahead,
'*Maybe I'm next! To Mumbai we've already so many jobs bled!*',
'*The country's so polarized as if it's only snowflake versus skinhead*',
'*I hope that bird flu outbreak won't into a global pandemic spread*',
To FoMO: '*Am I missing out if I do this instead?*',
On top of which, '*I must get 7 to 9 hours so by 11 I must be in bed*',

Our thoughts are gyrating when the world should be surreally abating,
And it's neither phones nor duvets nor thermostats we should be incriminating,
For it's an inescapable corollary of modern work and life—there's no debating,
For the mind once employed sans bodily fatigue prevailing,
Struggles to stop ruminating and agitating,
This is what we should be blaming for keeping us sleep waking.

Spree Thinker

'*Think for yourself*' to kids we blithely utter,
But if literally they lived it, we'd all shudder,

For here's all we really proffer:
Choices akin to—Coke or Pepsi? There's nothing more we offer,

An ostensible smorgasbord of options which dazzle to disguise,
The underlying homogeneity which we purport to despise,
Doing Goebbels proud, in hell as he fries,

Modern culture promises to defer:
'You do you'—we will not deter,
So long, of course, as the sky and earth are kept in place we will concur,

So when that rare philosopher kid climbs out of Plato's mall,
And witnesses the broad sunlight of freedom's sprawl,
Jittery—we fret—what will become of us all?
Institutions will collapse, democracy to family to economy will fall!

Not all at once, their tricks and mortar still strong,
First the most inane and insane frills to the cesspit of history where they belong,
You might even cheer for you long wanted only those gone,

But then, history warns—as always:
What's to stop their questioning rampaging through our hallowed hallways?

Until, as if from nowhere, the entire foundation shakes,
And along hitherto repressed fault lines polite society quakes,

But don't worry all epochs have known how fraught,
The dangers are of allowing free thought,
Ours is just different because in a big lie it is caught:
For from the other side of its mouth 'free thinking' is encouraged and taught,

Ours knows as much as its predecessors ever did that it ought,
To stop the free thinker at naught,
For free thinkers loosened from convention so taut,
Are spree thinkers who soon our world order to its knees would have brought.

InPracticality

'The elders', not all of them old, in one shrill voice would forebodingly decry,
'*Oh, why!? Oh why!?* they'd sigh,
Of my flights of fancy ever so skeptical,
They would admonish '*For your future's sake please be more PRACTICAL!*',
I didn't know why, but something told me their reasoning was awry,
Now, finally, I can reply:

Practicality just means that you're down with the prevailing regime,
For the ends that now reign supreme,
You're well-versed with the means to the extreme,
On the back of your hand tattooed the scheme,
This is all very well if all you want to achieve is the routine,
Wherein the stifling ceiling is already very much foreseen,

But I was captivated by the as yet undreamed,
For me a multiverse of futures gleamed,
As hitherto unfamiliar neural sparks teamed,
And an imagination smoothie streamed,
Oh modernity, even as creativity and innovation's praises you don't sing you scream,
How easily you forget that your today was but yesterday's daydream!

No matter propaganda's squeal,
Nor pretensions of free-wheeling zeal,
In any day and age, pragmatism always into dogmatism doth congeal,

Thereby, perversely and ironically, rendering practicality,
In the bigger picture long-term totality,
In actuality, a variety of impracticality,

For you see, if you don't set aside a bit of your self and time and mind,
Not only will you have no hope to find,
The next big thing of mankind,
But leaving such grandiosity to the rare mastermind,
More insidiously for the linear hence the myopically blind,
Given that change the only constant is ever so inclined,
To rot and even implode the tried-and-true that is currently designed,
Practical fundamentalists are likely not merely to be left behind,
But rudely shook when they meet their 'unforeseen' demise by a shock unkind,
Their fates flatlined,
Inpracticality their only would-be savior: the impracticality they so maligned.

Reel Dreams

I think it's pretty much common sense if you have a goal or a dream,
It's 'wisdom' which can even be gleaned from many a meme,
That you've gotta get off your ass and charge at it full steam,

For dreaming itself indulged in too deep and long,
Can be an act of procrastination so as to the comfy fantasizing stage prolong,

This is no novel insight for sure,
But here's where modern tech waylays with a delicious lure,

See anything that so captivates,
That the aforementioned fantasizing stage it too far elongates,
Your goals' or dreams' chances of realization this only attenuates,

To be clear,
I don't mean distractions besides the goal or dream material here,
And this is what makes them all the more tricky around to steer,
For the indulgence does not as wallowing in distraction seem or appear,
But indeed can be passed off as instrumental to achievement sincere,

Boy oh boy! Nowadays from your phone to your laptop,
Themed to your particular dream stream an endless crop,
Of delectable bite-sized morsels which like Pringles 'Once you pop,
You can't stop!',

The challenge posed to the doer is a function of and grows,
With the speed at which the insidious Internet at us these tidbits throws,
How slickly and provocatively their wares they propose,
And how bespoke to your aspirations they can pose,

And tis a formidable challenge like never before no doubt,
For one after another they whoosh at us—never a drought,
They're immaculately and irresistibly decked-out,
And they seem to be reading our minds just about,

The doer would be better served indeed,
If he had only his own imagination's apparition of his end-state to pay heed,
Along with to guide him some dry and difficult instructive material to read,

Herein was why literature was the great benefactor of the dreamer,
Whereas, it turns out that his great nemesis is the streamer,
For literature in contrast was relatively sparse and difficult and, yes, boring,
Sacrilegious I know so 'relatively' is worth underscoring,
Nevertheless, fair to say that the leap from the page to action,
Was large yet in comparison to the magnitude of stupefaction,
From hyper-consummate polished passive abstraction,
To jagged-edged hard-nosed arduous reality 'twas but a fraction,

Now I'm hours in viewing and viewing,
Convincing myself that this will help me better achieve what I am pursuing,
Perhaps what led me to them was that my performance anxiety got stewing,
I get it—this is akin to over and over the same cud chewing,
I know, I know—I should've started somewhere and got down to doing,
But these reel dreams are just so darn good at wooing.

Art Imitates

Always give the people what they want?
Well... perhaps in their government though that often comes back to haunt,
Definitely in most of their tastes—from their clothes to at a restaurant,

But from film and song to prose and verse,
And all other mediums diverse which the arts doth traverse,
Superior to straightforward and simple satisfaction—the converse:
Good art to democratization must stand averse,

See art can be many things:
Entertainment, escape... it can pull on your heartstrings,
As praises and woes it sings,
Even mud it slings,
But as well, it can bestow transcendent wings,

For it can liberate the man on the street,
From his cute conceit,
That his version of reality so neat and complete,
Is also everyone else's indeed and the one and only truth and way concrete,

And if he happens to be,
In a 'Matrix' of any variety,
True art has the pugnacious potentiality,
To make him aware that he is indeed under the jackboot of a hegemony,
Via a paradigm quaking awakening epiphany,

Now how is art to this achieve,
When the eccentric is disallowed to weave,
When the mad genius of his rightful role we wrongly relieve?

To the masses when we bequeath the license to 'conceive',
The best they can hope to circularly receive,
Is only that which from their pinhole camera they already perceive,
Further concreting their realism naive,

And worse, though many poor-mouth it a pet peeve,
When mediums to the hoi polloi artists are forced to leave,
In the basest way on the culture the masses defecate and heave,
Keeping up with the Kardashians in 'reality' make-believe,
Rotting their minds without reprieve,

So artist, the editor who has in too many focus groups dipped,
Then demands that with market insights your manuscript be chipped,
The executive who your script has flipped,
So sans Tibet 'your' movie to China can be shipped,
Anyone including yourself who has your artistic freedom stripped,
Remember, that tis not only yours but art's wings they have clipped,

I readily admit,
Pulp fiction in any age a hit,
But nowadays since everyone is digitally so close-knit,
It has never been more lucrative to the lowest common denominator solely submit,
Billions on earth—imagine in clits and tits the profit!
But when art imitates likes—it's shit!

Can't Spotify

Picture along an endless to the horizon high street,
Millions of ma-and-pa kiosks peddling their wares and every kind of treat,
And contesting against the pint-sized petite,
A behemoth big-box mart doth compete,

Now let's say the market is completely free,
That the sharks ostensibly let the guppies be,
This is akin to internet democracy,
Where any and all can upload their content unreservedly,
But herein imperceptibly,
The best artists are likely to suffer the worst,
For once creative democracy is unleashed it's their prospects which are cursed,

The high street shopper, the YouTube surfer in the boat same,
They cannot hope to parse each vendor of no-name,
There's simply too many millions in the game,
Of course they could randomly buy or click without aim,
But for us risk-averse humans arbitrariness is a strategy lame,
For what niggles us in the main—
What if our eeny-meeny-miny-moe selection sucks? How in vain!
The little guy tedious thus vexing,
The known-devil with their big-budget flexing,
Their brand name respecting,
The behemoth we end up selecting,

Now that one in a million makes it—shouldn't fool,
Careful of the survivorship bias: the overnight sensation over whom we drool,
Obscures all the perhaps even more talented drowned by the mediocre cesspool,
Thus such exceptions only prove the rule,

Now think what if the fence was much higher?
Far more talent and investments of all kinds were prerequisite to entry prior,
Certainly more than record and upload entry did require,
Then only the most talented would dare be a supplier,
For all but the most delusional tryer,
Being an also-ran—the costs and the risks would be way too dire,
This would in turn mean there'd be less from which to choose,
Hence each upstart's 'audition' we're more likely to peruse,
Thus less likely to wheat due to the chaff lose,
Less likely on the diamonds due to the riffraff snooze,
And now that they'd be going up against rivals their own size,
At least quality wise,
This would even the playing field—go a long way to rectify,
The unfair advantage of the behemoth from on high,
Over the genius we currently can't spotify.

Chore Adore

Tap of an app, push of a button,
Lo and behold—all of a sudden!
Laundry done, home sparkling clean, no need of the oven,
Yet hot food you'll be shovin',
With tedium at a min—life you'll be lovin',

'*Oh come on!*'—I hear you bray,
'*In this at least you can't poke holes—no freakin' way!*',
But alas, I must, albeit with dismay,

You see, chores by definition are so mindless and boring,
That your mind hence, almost snoring,
Is let loose to go exploring,

If we were to our neuroscience caps don:
With nothing difficult to concentrate upon,
The 'Default Mode Network' is turned on,

'*So what!?* you may dismissively ask why,
But here there's much more than meets the eye,

In this vague wayfaring state,
Diverse species of thought that you'd consciously never relate,
Can by strange twists of neural fate,
Bump into each other then date,

Then mate,
Then procreate,

Their offspring: unicorns and chimera—voila!
There you are—EUREKA!

To this end the monomania of work and life won't sufficiently allow askew,
Deadlines due,
Clients pursue,
Boss always behind you,
Bills, troubles, worries and anxieties accrue,
All keep you too hyper-focused: blinders on, tunnel vision—nothing else in view,

But chores are the sweet spot,
Stress? Rarely a lot,
No biggie if say you forgot,
And—oops!—let the groceries rot,
Your fingers on the nuclear trigger are not,
Chores are chill enough on the dot,
To let you safely wander off from the plot,

And what of all that 'Me time' gadgets were supposed to afford?
Well, far from being creatively bored,
Yet more gadgets will this time only hoard,
Peel your eyes away from your phone—by the blahs you won't be floored,
TVs to watches to gaming devices—modern life spent over smart devices pored,

Soon when even that great incubator of 'Aha!'—the shower,
Like in the Jetsons dour efficiency does devour,
Creativity our very human superpower,
Which above all else doth tower,
Will find less soil to flower,

Perhaps, for creativity's sake at least modern conveniences galore,
Which if not abhor,
We should wish to have less—not more,
Whilst tis the good ole chore we should adore.

Nice Pollution

Tis maybe true of your favorite food or song,
That if you indulge every day and for too long,
Meh—it habituates—some of the whiz-bang is gone,

For such things, the profane, variety truly is the spice,
This analogy though simple and nice,
From the perspective of your life's paramount pursuit tis bad advice,
And to explicate it another analogy doth suffice,

Think your passion a delicacy not of this world but divine,
So sacred and sublime which, as such, tis so delicate and fine,
That if your palette you sully with the merely nice and sometimes saccharine,
You have denied yourself the timeless transcendence of the holy wine,

Modern life a smorgasbord,
Chock-a-block with innumerable nice things that more and more can afford,
Which I heedlessly hanker to hoard,
Inconsiderate of that which my soul always adored,

A smartphone in every pocket, a TV in every abode,
A new Italian place has opened up just down the road,
Pics of my trips to upload,
Oh ya, there's the reminder—better get into yoga mode,

My time, my money, my energy all spent,
Maintaining this merry-go-round of meh—I'm stressed, I'm discontent,

I've spread myself thin to such an extent,
My passions which once the world to me meant,
I can't even remember the last time of them I've dreamt,

Nice pollution—it's sure to circumvent and disorient,
And tis ultimately a tributary to modernity's vapid torment.

Cloy Ploy

''*Cause today I don't feel like doing anything...*' so as the song doth tout,
Get those 'sweat' pants and chips and dips out,
Slob on the couch, workout regime flout,
Voyeur as those Insta influencers pout,

Pass the goss along the grapevine,
Hate-scroll down your ex's timeline,
Jack-off to porn—it's no crime, you're fine,

But be forewarned: tis by struggling up the Sisyphean hill, and only therein,
Can man ever hope to meaning win,
Quit at the gift shop before you even begin,
And a growling emptiness will soon churn into chagrin,

For any pleasure instant and visceral only,
First luscious dollop delish, but soon—sickly sweet—phony baloney,
Over-indulge—you'll get dumped leaving you existentially lonely,

So instant gratification akin to downing a whole bottle of liquor,
We've all been there with a hangover never having felt sicker,
But how exactly does it existential fulfilment deter?
The answer I'm tempted to cheekily but fittingly defer,
But nay, nay I shall aver not demur,

See creature comforts and lowbrow entertainment their irresistibility,
Lies in their devilish ability,
To provide pleasure with passivity,
In, admittedly, doing so with expert effectivity,
They thereby contemporaneously,
Glibly alienate me simultaneously,
Precisely, by denying me what should be my sacrosanct opportunity,
To self-actualizingly paint creatively with the water colors of my individuality,
Thus disenfranchising my generative faculty,
Which is integral to the flowering of my humanity,

And all this, the evidence is in, doesn't just happen unintentionally willy-nilly,
From social media to fast-food giants to Big Pharma types like Eli Lilly,
It's a feature not a bug,
Hiring psychologists to neuroscientists everything is designed to be a drug,
To keep you physically and intellectually snug,

So buyer beware of Brave New World-esque manufactured joy,
Like a gift horse into Troy,
Tis but an insidious cloy ploy.

Homo Maker

At the end of a long hard day,
Or when I get to exhale: '*Thank god it's Friday!*',
To put my feet up I've earned the right, I'd say,

But with apologies for being a wet blankey,
Those empty calories and pixels that tempt thee,
Devour—and the gluttony will leave you empty,

See, you think you are exhausted and drained,
But it goes commonly unexplained,
That oft tis only your body you have strained,
And only your willpower for serfdom you have waned,

Rest assured your transcendent energies don't just remain,
Like subdued champagne,
If shaken—POP!—right off the top goes the cork that hitherto did restrain,
Lavishing a glorious reign,

Awe, curiosity, surreality, spontaneity, fantasy, ingenuity, originality,
Bubble ever so ebulliently,
To this world be born in an Archimedean eureka epiphany as creativity,
To transubstantiate your élan vital into reality,

This 'Chi' that inspires man to be more than the easel and the canvas merely,
To color with his imagination painterly,

Cannot be unleashed by indulgences solely lowly,
Certainly not by creature comfort and lowest-common-denominator insipidity,

And, all the more magically,
To daily drudgery,
It works oppositely,
The more one imbibes from its well thirstily,
The quicker its aqua vitae replenishes rapidly,

Indeed, when its waters are forsaken only,
When you're browbeaten by monotony,
Then you consequently succumb to vegetative passivity,
Does this well dry up—deserted and dreary,
Leaving you existentially quagmired in a blackhole of banality,

So on holidays and after each workday when you quit,
To your highest calling recommit,
Make something in your own image with all of you invested in it,
Which your crown as creator doth befit,

Don't be decoyed by the cloy ploy, 'Homo Faber',
Be God on this earth—be 'Man the Maker'.

Ew! Morality

Two men anally penetrating,
Polyamorous gang-bangs fornicating taking turns fellating,
Trans-gender genital mutilating,
Dicks in women's toilets urinating,
Pristine pre-teen tots with puberty blockers nature adulterating,
Babies baying for life in the womb their tomb asphyxiating,
These visions can be viscerally disgusting, nauseating,
There's no debating,

And not just for the home-spun hick, the pious prude, the conservative shrew,
But, own up, in flashes even for the woke and me too,

But we mustn't judge nor overreact,
Think of their revulsion as exact,
To yours if made to picture mom and dad in the act,

Tis only when your higher-order mental faculties come online,
You can reconcile: what you just saw is natural and healthy therefore totally fine,
And this takes time for reason is a guru who resides up a steep incline,

Now if it's so slow and vexatious for you to get over mom giving dad oral,
Even given that you consider the said act perfectly moral,
You can imagine the Herculean struggle and quarrel,
Required to win over those who judge a behavior abominable and immoral,

So keep top of mind that reflex disgust,
In order to be flushed and to the dustbin of history be thrust,
Baby steps with hand-holding all along the way is an absolute must,

If deplored as ignorant, backward and vile,
If we don't proceed prudently with guile,
'They' will dig in their heels—defensive and hostile,

Then far from opening 'their' eyes to the inclusive dawn of a new morality,
We'll have forever condemned 'them' to the darkness of ew! morality.

Drudge Fudge

Poor, middle-class, rich,
Somewhat trite—so this distinction let's ditch,
For another though which,
Is as much clinical economic outcomes' bitch,
To winner, loser, drudger let's switch,

A loser is anyone who,
Though it may not be their own fault—true,
Via only their own efforts through,
Cannot their basic needs attend to,
Food on the table,
Clothes on their back, roof over their heads—they're not able,

Though both drudgers and winners of self-sufficiency are well capable,
The contrast between them is inescapable,

See to the winner's wills their realities bend,
For on them their worlds' fates seem to depend,

For the high-and-mighty by definition this has always been so,
They may nowadays appear in some modern incarnations though:
The celebrity, the sports star, the CEO,
In even the lucky lottery winner you can throw,
Yet nothing has changed—hell no,
As long as they don't get caught doing something criminal or abominably low,

Perched atop the status quo,
They can do pretty much as they please—march to the beat of their own banjo,
Little, if any, explanation do they owe,
Their sovereignty is way, way more than the drudgers below,

On their hamster wheels relentlessly running the rat-race,
Modern tech only accelerating the pace,
Offering no refuge, no hiding place,
Autonomy and creativity though management assures it doth embrace,
Mostly it's lip-service and teasing with just enough of a trace,
Bread-crumbing drudgers to keep up the chase,

Again—but hasn't this always been the case?

Yes, but it's not at the workplace that the drudgers' fate has been remade,
It's in the charade on them that modern culture has played,
By managing to persuade,
That there's none such as a drudger—so never be dismayed,
You are a winner on your very own glorious crusade!
So of course walk the walk and dress the part,
With the winner's regalia fill up your shopping cart,

But apart from consumerism that dark art,
This is pernicious to the psyche and the heart,

For when the autonomy and all else that's 'rightfully' yours the universe doth begrudge,
When your reality won't budge,
To the self-image that modern man can't help but clutch,
It can hurt so much,

So better not your lot misjudge—
Better not fall for the drudge fudge.

Naughtonomy

Imagine yourself a child,
Upon whom inspiration has smiled,

A project completed,
Or at a contest succeeded,
Or a new skill seeded,
Or a personal best superseded,

So to impress mom and dad you run conceited,
But alas each and every time you end up defeated,

Your perennial arch-nemesis—an older sibling,
Who being better than you at everything, all the while whistling,
Leaves you bristling,

This fate is akin,
To a predicament within modern life we find ourselves in,

The amateur's naïve zeal,
With his own 'recipe' to cook a Michelin Star meal,
To shape his life's clay in any which way he may feel,
Is soon assailed, and must deal,
With the beckoning of pro foes who will not yield and so make him reel,

There's always a better way, and it's off-the-rack,
For the code has already been cracked by specialists with the knack,
But if you just YouTube or Google a hack,
You start by seeking self-efficacy but end up feeling like a quack,

And feelings aside,
Quite a dilemma is implied,
Between a rock and an easy place—the amateur must decide,

If on your own course you stubbornly embark,
Get ready for a lot of fiddling around in the dark,

But follow the way of the consummate pro,
For the quick fix of efficiency and quality that it definitely does bestow,
And you may be surrendering much more though,
For tis your autonomy you must let go,

And this is no readily recoupable right to give away,
For needless to say,
At work too we are told what to do and how to do it—and we must obey,

Oh amateur, you're in an unenviable pickle you see,
For at your fingertips many a past-master community,
That save for a stroke of genius, rare even for those with the most ingenuity,
Are infinitely better than humble hobbyists like you and me,
So as opposed to standing on my own two feet indy and free,
I tap or click on the apps of the savvy— irresistibly easy-peasy!

Wonder though what in the long-run the toll will be on creativity,
Can't imagine it will impregnate imaginative biodiversity,
How could it when there's a centralized top-down homogeneity?
Devilish but not really a difficult dichotomy:
On the daily, who really cares about creativity and autonomy?
Oh modernity how you expertly coax me into naughtonomy!

Dream On

Never in history before,
Has the individual's dreams mattered more,
Follow them relentlessly modernity doth implore,
And there's absolutely nothing wrong with this—I must underscore,

But there is something the dreamer ought know for it lies in store,
Though convenient for the propagandists to ignore:
The sweat, blood and tears you the dreamer pour—
Tis the market price of your dream—of swinging open the golden door,

Hence it must follow,
That the forces of supply and demand apply so:
Dreamers like you more and more—then up and up the price must go,
For each's ardor sets the bar higher and higher with no sign of plateau,
Yet even if prices soar, for the dreamer small matter though,
Tis but a tuppence to bask in transcendence's glorious glow,

The thornier truth, though, goes right to dreaming's philosophical core,
Why do dreams enrapture us so? Let's explore:
Tis not only that they are the culmination of the self-actualization we so adore,
Tis as much that rare indeed it is to set foot upon the promised land's shore,
So say if, lo and behold, every dream of every dreamer came true heretofore,
Would the next captivate us anymore?
No—realizing your dreams would be quite the bore akin to completing a chore,

'*There's a broken heart for every light on Broadway*' so the song goes,
More like a million I would interpose,
Dream but don't '*...make dreams your master*'—Kipling was right I suppose,
Yet, dreamer dream on—I propose,
Not because with perseverance your odds grow or you might get lucky—who knows!?
But because an unfulfilled dream inflicted woes,
Pale next to the undreaming soul's nihilistic death throes.

Alive & Killing

How does the world work? How does it go around?
The answer—each self-important ideology doth resound:
'That I and only I have found',
Then hurriedly its paradigm it doth expound,
And soon licks its lips desirous to gain ground,
Ambitious to remake the world in its likeness and have itself crowned,

Organized religion ideology's oldest kind,
'Twas expertly designed,
For all its decrees: absurd or cruel or benign never mind,
It placed the wrath of the almighty behind,

But the Enlightenment came,
To expose religion's game,
With the light of reason darkness disclaim,
Then both history and the future Marxism tried to reframe,
But human nature being still at a nascent developmental stage it couldn't tame,
Which meant that its revolutionary flame,
Would rapidly wane—such a shame,

In the vacuum, consumerism laid claim,
Though unlike its predecessors not seeking to explain nor blame,
But just like its cousins before it took aim,
To the world in its own image ordain—in that way all ideology the same,

And some were cocksure that this did portend,
That history itself would come to an end,
Ah, but little did they comprehend,

See consumerism's hegemony is built on a shaky foundation unsound,
For capitalism by its nature is topsy-turvy: skyrocketing high then crashing earthbound,
So when the roaring good times are by recession or depression inevitably drowned,
When from consumerism's teat succor doth not abound,
The addicts craving, resentful, tightly wound,
Are to fall prey bound,
To the most hateful and disastrous ideologies which cynically hound,

No 1929 Wall Street Crash,
Hitler—in the pan but a flash,

2008 Financial Crisis,
Trump had the sheeple believe that Obama founded ISIS,

Blue collar jobs lost to the Poles,
Brexit machinated by Boris and his trolls,

German welfare state strained by an influx of refugees,
To the Bundestag elected neo-Nazis,

This truth the CCP and Xi Jinping well knows,
Even Winnie the Pooh censored—ever vigilant on their toes,
For as economic growth slows,
Against them will rise ideological foes,

And there's another reason that must be told,
For it too weakens consumerism's hold,
See for some in the conservative Third World not in consumerism's fold,
All that glitters is not always gold,

In fact, opposite indeed,
Often consumerism is perceived with its wanton hedonism and greed,
As a debauched and corrupting creed,
A neo-imperialist enterprise that must not be allowed to succeed,

Traditional garb and grub—nah, jeans and Big Macs and Coke is all we need,
When hip-hop profanity and Nintendo Switch so bewitch, though we plead,
How can we get them to quaint rites and rituals accede?
Not deference to elders but only celebrities and influencers they heed,
Bikini clad models selling legalized weed,
Porn at kids' finger-taps on their social media feed,
Too much, too soon at too fast a speed,
Antagonist ideologies—the Al-Qaedas and the Talibans—breed,

Ideology is not dead—hell no!
Nor has it been given any kind of deathblow,
Nor has one all others managed to forever overthrow,
Tis only so,
The only difference being faster than before, though,
For the modern world is anything but slow,
That in a not-so-merry-go-round they come and go and ebb and flow,

On this earth for as long as man is living and has top-billing,
He can't merely be going-through-the motions treadmilling,
He needs meaning, purpose and structure for life to be fulfilling,
Enter ideology—some of them chilling,
This role it's always been filling,
And tis still ever willing,
Ideology is very much alive and killing.

Modern Taboo

The very definition of a minority,
Should be that now or in history,
It's a group which faces or faced discrimination or some atrocity,

Black people to the two millennia hatred of the Jew,
LGBTQ to women, Red Indians, Asians even Italians—the definition holds true,

The last 500 years-ish—let's not tiptoe,
Have been dominated by straight white men so...
From the Inca and Aztec overthrow,
The Jewish Ghetto,
Colonial plunder and its long shadow,
Slavery through Jim Crow,
A woman's place is in the home or at most for the same work getting paid low,
'Don't Ask, Don't Tell' to the covert country club—NO!
We all know how the story goes cringe blow by blow,

But oh how, oh how as the subjugated,
Have become ever more emancipated,
Their legit critics they have so castrated,

Of their cultures and subcultures, values and norms fearing the kitchen sink,
One dare not critically even think,
Let alone point out even the slightest chink,
For—racist!/sexist!/prejudiced!—forever will follow you the stink,
This cancer in the culture will cancel you in a blink,

But how has this come to pass an about-face of the bad ole past?
How have the tables turned 180° so fast?

See all it took was to capitalize on the human conscience inbuilt,
Point out to the unrelenting hilt,
That for the centuries of oppression under whose jackboot minorities did wilt,
There ought to be commensurate White guilt,

So it's not even up for discussion:
Absentee Black fatherhood so crushin',
Work and motherhood—the repercussion,
Gender fluidity—are we pushin'?

But don't think for this counter-suppression there won't be a white-lash,
Embodied in Trump it's already afoot, and not only from the White Trash,
Sufferin' succotash!
Why surprised when reasonable concerns and queries you dash?
When you sequester them to fester in the dark corners of the web—newsflash:
It's just a matter of time until your pity party they violently crash,
And your snowflake idols they smash!

Wonder what progress we could accrue,
If to overcompensation we do not hew,
If we let a vigorous and rigorous debate ensue,
For reparations not the emperor's new clothes in lieu,
If the quest for truth we do not throttle—we proactively pursue,
If we do not declare it a no-go, no-no—a modern taboo we must eschew.

Sexual Devolution

Sex—threesome the provenance of its gratification,
A good fuck's carnal flesh-on-flesh titillation,
Making love—two hearts never closer in intimate pulsation,
But the third—only if a taboo prevails against fornication,

Ah, to do what they say you never should,
Oh Eve, the dishonors if you would,
Forbidden fruit tastes so, so good!

So back when pre-marital sex was taboo,
'Twas not as if lovers fornication did eschew,
Of course they did screw,
And 'twas all the headier too,
Drunk on illicit devil's brew,

Come the Sexual Revolution,
This naughtiness received absolution,
But a kink mainstreamed spells if not its conclusion then at least its dilution,

So the former pre-marital fornicators,
Freed now by the moral legislators,
Were left with only two pleasure generators,

Since love—rare—its provenance numinous alchemy,
In motion and mechanics fleshly,

And moans and groans of sextasy,
Former fornicators came to rely sexclusively,

Want to learn its best-practice and skills?
Playboy and Cosmo teach you drills,
Pornhub and xHamster make you wanna pop pills,
Sex and the City sensationalizes its spills and its thrills,

But as performers under pressure will attest,
Sometimes when the body by the mind is hard-pressed,
Things can go south—contrary to what we request,
Thus this foreskin-deep carnal quest,
Mind-blowing orgasm its holy grail, its climactic acid test,
Is a precarious versus the self contest,
And since anticipated pleasure's or pain's intensity is always less than we guessed,
Such sex is fated to be 'meh' at best,

Oh such an anti-climax when the Sexual Revolution's bequest:
Sexual devolution—chokes pleasure with our own bodily behest.

Hetro Detraction

Damsel in distress,
Or kittenishly twirling a tress,
Waiting for you—and you alone—her knight in shining armor to undress,

She shan't be heard only seen,
Coveted as she dutifully doth cook and clean,
Belonging in your shadow demure and serene,

And even if she got beat,
She had to wince with broken teeth but smile and greet,
Perhaps it was for her own good and not to ill-treat,
Besides these things happen in love so bittersweet,

Her rightful role to 'ascend' to the throne of your nurturing mother queen,
'The Second Sex' de Beauvoir I so get what you mean,
Fertile soil for your seed,
Woman—made in the image of man's need,

But freed of the delusions of male hegemony here's the real deal:
She's as good at math and science—tis no longer a big reveal,
She graduates from high school and college at a rate that makes boys reel,
She's better at work and can lead though she's still hardly given the wheel,
So, perhaps, it's only fair your job she should 'steal',
Yet as the once binary gender roles melt fluidly and congeal,
We've got to begrudgingly concede,
That the attraction between opposites must necessarily recede,

For where's the complementary other half Plato claimed we all seek?
The yin to your yang—so to speak,
Venus and Mars in a rhythmic two-to-tango drumbeat,
Male advance and female retreat,
Which in a coruscating carousel of passion's heat,
Eternally revolves, full circle, from machismo's conceit,
To masculinity worshipping at femininity's feet,

Oh spare me woke thought police please,
But nowadays straight relationships are so hard to maintain geez!
And one reason among many with which even I'm ill at ease,
Is that at loggerheads clash two male energies,
Repelling as do like magnetic poles—negating sexually charged synergies,

Humans are the heretics of nature—I agree,
So no natural and certainly no cultural decree,
Abide by need we,
And with feminism the reasonable cannot reasonably disagree,
But, undeniably, from hetero attraction a subtraction is plain to see,
A hetero detraction brought on by a modernity where progressively she is he.

Occidental Chameleon

Four sibling chameleons go each their own way,
To four forests each very different from the other in lands far, far away,

They blend in as chameleons are adapted to do,
Some green, some red, some blue,
All to their adopted forest true,

As time goes by,
Different survival strategies each camouflage of chameleons try,

The harsher, the more unforgiving their forest's terrain,
The more precarious life is to sustain,
Forged by ever impending death and pain,
To survive they must industriously employ their brain,

Whereas, their kin in forests more salubrious,
Have no such survival imperative to be so studious,
They can afford a little more insouciance—they needn't be as duteous,

Those who have it easy—at the starting gun ahead,
Their first foray to survive then thrive by natural endowment bred,
In the race of life to the front of the pack though they well may have sped,

They will soon be surpassed,
For those who had to overcome challenges vast,

Each generation building on the compulsory enlightenment of the last,
Find that a treasure of skills, knowledge and technologies they have amassed,

And, here's the hopeful glint: these invaluable lessons learned,
Not only beneficent for those who've them by toil and error hard-earned,
But can be equally so for all concerned,

So 'twould be such a pitiful shame,
If chameleon kin far and yonder upon mere fleeting colors disclaim,
This heritage of the entire chameleon race—for beneath all are the same,

Especially given that if the paths which each camouflage initially traversed,
Were reversed,
The very same difference would result—but only inversed,

And, the day may very well come,
When sunny salubriousness into treacherous terrain does become,
And the 'last' are survival-pressured to evolve into the 'first' lest they succumb,

Perhaps circumstance in the last half-millennia may have hard-pressed,
The occidental chameleon to have learnt most and best,
But chameleon kin North, East, South, West,
Do not each consider yourself apart from the rest,
In the arbitrary and superficial divest,
Of your whole race's heritage choose not to be dispossessed,
Embrace—for all can be blessed.

Home Alone

The child truly becomes an adult—reaches their majority,
Aside from legally, not when they turn 18 merely,
But really when to take care of themselves they develop the ability,
Only then should they, deservingly, be granted over their affairs sovereignty,

Thusly, to preempt torment,
We dare not leave a toddler unattended for nary a moment for disaster it may portent,
The stove into a conflagration they may well foment,

Analogously, the same logic you see,
Holds true for our much-vaunted democracy,

'Twas decades ago,
When the colonial foe,
Whether because of the world war near deathblow,
Or the independence struggle heave-ho,
Begrudgingly, their former fiefdoms had to let go,

Centuries of pillaging and plunder—I know,
And plantation economies and neo-imperialism—exploitative although,
To the post-colonial rot, if not implosion, there is a deeper cause below,

Remember how Hiroshima and Nagasaki were apocalyptically consumed whole,
And on Japan the human, material and psychological toll,
Yet, how from the ashes the 'Land of the Rising Sun' with a singular goal,

Did Western industry steamroll?
For this miracle tis Japanese values and virtues we must credit and extoll,
See tis not that from Conquistadors to the Dutch VOC, diamonds to coal,
From Indo-China to Africa the French and the British Raj stole,
What is to blame is none other than the Third World soul,

Petty-minded and pathologically plagued by the Tall Poppy Syndrome,
Sees no need to plan—with chaos very much at home,
With superficial status so obsessed—substance by the wayside thrown,
Anti-intellectuals whom at abstraction groan,
Dishonest and duplicitous, manipulative and to suspicion prone,
Rules and laws obeying in abeyance alone,
Unapologetically insular and nepotistic favoring only their own,
And most cancerously of all—corrupt to the bone,

Hold on! Before the 'White Man's Burden' we hasten to invoke,
Tis not race that is the Third World malaise's yoke,
But rather the pre-modern cultural DNA that damn the black and brown folk,

So when bundled with independence democracy is granted in a pen stroke,
Tis but giving children the vote—tis fate we doth provoke,
Leaving them home alone—can you smell the smoke?

Hmm... Maturity

What really is immaturity?
'Tis but one's inability,
To resist the temptation of instant gratification—that very human fallibility,
And pursue a course of action which in all calculable probability,
Will yield the best chance of maximizing one's long-term utility,

Picture a kid à la Augustus Gloop gobbling and gulping the entire candy store,
Who ends up with cavernous cavities galore,
Or by losing it with your boss in a raging roar,
Saying bye-bye to that promotion and raise—nevermore!

But culture cleverly espouses maturity using it as a bait-and-switch Trojan horse,
In the guise, 'This is all for your own good'—of course,
It surreptitiously conflates maturity with conformity,
And before you know it you're reality deep in absurdity,

Take our word for it—'Stay on the straight-and-narrow'—keep grinding,
Over the calculus your weary mind you needn't wring,
Thusly, maturity is decoupled from that which future reward to you doth bring,

When your sacrifices are not for you but to keep the system's wheels turning,
Via keeping up the appearances to which you're enculturated to cling,
Maturity hath become mindlessly doing the done thing,

Anything to enhance my lot,
More so to show—look what I've got!
So I take out a second mortgage to swing clubs—both country and yacht,
Even loving my spouse—about that it is not,
But ending up a cliché divorcé(e)—anything to avoid that blot,
That's only why I'm giving couples therapy a shot,
Never mind that the stress is causing my back to knot,
About my own kids I know diddly-squat,
Duh, they resent me—I don't remember their last birthday I haven't forgot,
All the while ever hardens that arterial blood clot,

I wish I hadn't just hung up my college degree merely ceremoniously,
I could've figured out the smart thing for me—on my own—individually,
All I would've needed is the courage to pursue it bullheadedly,

'Maturity' is ever on a military-esque grown-up recruitment spree,
It's been boot-camping me into shipshape from when I was wee,
Turns out it wasn't temptation that I couldn't resist—but orthodoxy, you see,
And its nemesis, in this incarnation at least—'immaturity'—just means to a tee,
You're not serving the powers-that-be,
Hmm...maturity—you never really gave a shit about me!

Identity Carnard

Am I country, am I race, am I religion, am I gender, am I family? Who am I?
Now classical liberals may decry,
These as otherwise arbitrary labels which lead us dangerously awry,
Only imposed for the expediency of the patriarchy so we mustn't comply,
Though I get it, I do—but call me old-fashioned with these I yet identify,

And here's why:
From scratch to make and remake myself when I try,
From whichever caterpillar become my own butterfly,
Other than, of course, it being much harder work, none can deny,
Than the 'fast-food' version of identity off-the-shelf opting to buy,
I've gotta fight a trio of more formidable foes if I'm fashioning myself on the fly,

Firstly, group membership is 'batteries included', you see,
When I don the group's identity,
My life choices are pre-validated by my fellow in-group fraternity,
Whereas, strike out on my own—second-guessing an inevitability,
I'll have to 'purchase' validation separately,

And secondly, the weight of my world will rest on my shoulders squarely,
For unlike the self-images of my tribes which unwarrantedly,
Preen toward the extreme of immaculacy delusionally,
Crowned with a grandiosity,
Encrusted with the cherry-picked best from amongst the millions of my coterie,
Me with my faults and failures—my all too human fallibility,

Will be left to derive my self-image far more, if not totally,
From stone-cold reality,
And since now my identity = only me, I could end up writhing in egoistic anxiety,

Thirdly, and most gravely,
Individuality pits me against my own mortality,
Later than sooner I hope, but I have to die eventually,
Yet my groups will outlive me seemingly for eternity,
And therein I feel not corporeally but spiritually,
I will live on indefinitely,
My group identity is the guarantee of my immortality,

Nazism, racism, fascism, sexism—every bad -ism,
The bloody barbarity of history and of untold 21st Century cataclysm,
The madness of crowds fulminating into a January 6th paroxysm,
All different wavelengths of otherism,
Refracted through the same identity prism,
We should really give it the boot—render it an anachronism,
No matter how natural it may be we shouldn't be held back by essentialism,
Too bad then—what a diabolism,
That the identity canard is such an effective vaccine against nihilism.

Objectdeified

One to another we are taught never to objectify,
For doing so is to a subject's very humanity deny,

But sometimes, at least, we shouldn't scamper away shy,
And here's why:

An object we like for one or more quality,
Whether puppies for their playful jollity,
Or the Civil Rights Movement for pursuing racial equality,
Or democracy for expressing plurality,
Or smart phones for their convenient connectivity,
Or porn for its carnality,
The actuation of this quality—that's all we want from them in totality,

Whereas of our fellow subject we know verily of all their capacious capabilities,
That beyond their qualities and proclivities,
That they are possessed of consciousness hence a fertility of possibilities,

So to our friends and family,
And our partners especially,
We look to ever so expectantly,
For that which we seek, that je ne sais quoi—exactly,
To flow forth the very moment we seek it, precisely,
No pressure! Indubitably!

And when they can't live up, inevitably,
We hurt and in backlash bicker, inexorably,

We're like Moses striking the rock twice when we lose our objectivity,
And demand more and more from our nearest-and-dearests' subjectivity,

In contrast, whereas even when our playful pup chews,
Our brand-spanking new shoes,
Or our team finally wins—the hangover from all that booze,
Or the latest episode of our favorite show was a bit of a snooze,
Or our trusty old car to start does refuse,
We scarcely consider to with animus them accuse,

Alas, here then the root of many a relationship blues,
To nip before even the bud instead this mindset use:
So long as the subject whose—
Qualities I once loved and hence pursued,
Is with the self-same qualities still imbued,
I'm better off swimming against this modern tide,
Which insists that my lover must be my Swiss army knife alpha-and-omega bona fide,
Or else I'm being deprived and denied,
For I need a check against my expectations else multiplied,
I need to recast my partner, celestial eyed,
As once more the shining knight, the blushing bride,
The object of my affection sanctified,
The subject objectdeified.

Love Bug

Hollywood to Bollywood,
Valentine's Day the Big Bad Wolf to your Red Riding Hood,
Culture convincing you that falling in love is a garden-variety good,
Just hang in there—believe!—and find it you should,

Swipe left, swipe right in search of a spark to ignite,
Basement dwelling momma's boys or hairy upper lips in spite,
Demand love—after all, it is a human right,
And don't you ever give up the good fight,

Many fall in love—indeed,
Some do stay in love—I'll readily concede,
But for everyone to expect to—whoa, whoa!—now there's the big mislead,

It's a very modern claim right up there with the bait-and-bewitch of fame,
Tinder may compromise long-term love with its hit-it-and-quit-it game,
And despite your fumbles on Bumble, it's not apps you should blame,
When you're expecting a 'Notebook' kinda flame,
But 'love' actually—if you find it—tis in comparison lame,

Regardless how the monolithic mantra goes,
Even they didn't make it—some just aren't lucky enough to be Jack & Rose,
For some would-be soul mates their orbits may have come tantalizingly close,
At that wedding or in the very next apartment building—who knows?
But it just wasn't meant to be—karma—some may conveniently suppose,

And some are at heart single,
And some, if they're being honest, prefer to 'mingle',
They don't need Big Cupid to manufactured dissatisfaction sprinkle,
Bugging them—find 'the one and only' for whom your heart must twinkle,

Lonely but can't find Cinderella or Prince Charming?
Here's what's heartening, though to modern ears alarming:
To cure loneliness you can make do without your perfect darlin',
Settling: what's the harm in?

American Obituary

Though the Republic and democracy, Caesar and Augustus still recent in memory,
The Pax Romana and the glory of 'Roma Caput Mundi' seemed like a reverie,

For Commodus to Elagabalus portended,
That Rome '*From a kingdom of gold to one of iron and rust*' as Dio contended,
Was an empire whose dominance would soon be ignominiously ended,

The rich drunk on bacchanalia and hubris mollified,
The poor on whom the whole house of cards relied,
With rhetoric and propaganda which the iniquities and inequities sanctified,
And 'bread and circuses' which kept them distracted and preoccupied,
Such that 'twas too late by the time the rot from inside was popularly decried,

And whenever the earth beneath the empire did perilously tremor and grate,
The patrician class their responsibility were quick to abdicate:
Those barbarians at the gate!
The scapegoats the plebs were indoctrinated to hate,

That this doesn't have an ominous ring of familiarity,
Blah-blah—the wealthiest nation in history reeking of poverty,
Its trillion dollar military,
Brought to its knees by 'terrorist masterminds' with just fertilizer and a battery,
With healthcare in the 'Land of the Free',
Coming at an extortionist fee,
Civility and its value-system degenerating terminally,
Its standing in the world declining precipitously,

Ya-ya, yada-yada but it is what it is, and I'm just too busy so leave me be,
Keeping up with the Kardashians on E!
And with my hustle I'm the one that's gonna make it just you see,

As a symptom of this life stage of empire's decay:
A 'billionaire' jumped out from the screens of a reality TV stage play,

Who forget being an apprentice,
In statecraft—unlike in golden showers of piss,
Was and is a dotarded novice,

His debauchery flaunting not even trying to conceal,
With brazen demagoguery touting his 'Art of the Deal',
Promising to build a wall that'd the borders seal,
To the racists and basest appeal,
Not out of nowhere, though in 2016 unreal it did feel,
From the establishment the election he unwittingly did steal,

Trump, yes a symptom but also in turn a subsequent cause of the decline,
In a vicious cycle that will this once preeminent sole superpower consign,
To the sty of Third World swine,

And sooner than you expect will come to pass modern Rome's plight,
Given outside its borders China's burgeoning might,
Britain's ill-advised flight,
Putin's psychopathic smite,
The fundamentalist's unabating spite,
And the climate inferno Trump will unrepentantly only incite,

That Trump's an anti-hero à la Nero, and the whole Roman parallel though trite,
No other analogy can cast better diagnostic light,
On this great nation's cancerous blight,

And like with the palace intrigues of global empires past—the world holds its breath,
But unlike before, it's a question of life and literally sudden death,

For the megalomaniacal narcissist's tiny fingers on the nuclear trigger,
Are more experienced on Twitter! The stakes for humanity could not be bigger!

Way too dramatic and dire?
But before you dismiss this as just sore-loser liberal ire,
You have to concede at least that history repeating itself does regularly transpire,
And nothing lasts forever—that's sure-fire,

So you'd have to accept at the bare minimum in theory:
The election of Donald Trump might have marked the end of the American Century,
And that his re-election might mean we'd better start planning her funerary,
So historians and scholars should start writing the American obituary.

Crown Frown

When reason usurped God from 'his' throne rippled many a repercussion,
Most of them positive no doubt, no need of discussion,

But '*Heavy lies the head...*' oh my!—this the hard way we've found,
No matter that 'he' was never up there nor all around,
For as long as 'he' had a plan for you—this was the greatest solace profound,

But now, fair and square, by a hefty burden on my shoulders I am downed,
For I cannot look up when my best laid plans run aground,
'Life's full of ups and downs' and other such clichés though abound,
And self-help quacks for-profit feel-good inanities expound,
In my heart of hearts, these are but small mercies which scarcely resound,

As Dylan sang, '*Advertising signs they con you into thinking you're the one...*',
'*That can do what's never been done...*',
'*That can win what's never been won*',
Of the zeitgeist how spot-on!

Life revolves around me—I'm the sun,
But with great power comes a great responsibility which I dare not shun,
From which modernity will never let me run,

For if I do retreat,
It just means I couldn't handle the kitchen's heat,
I'm not good enough—life has me beat,

Leaving me a loser downbeat,
So there's no way on Earth I can concede defeat,

See of me the average joe than in any time in history before,
Is expected so, so much more,
This only compounds my multifarious modern misery and in this vortex I drown,
I'm a modern monarch donning a crown frown.

Downsmart

In nature which 'A' causes which 'B',
When man learns to clearly see,
From here springs many of the marvels of modernity,

We no longer needed to pray and wait for god 'his' magic wand to wave,
For when we figured out that it's our double helix DNA which to us life gave,
How to bacteria stave,
How the atoms and elements behave,
From the billions of lives we managed to save,
To the creature comforts and gadgets which we crave,
To the moon landing—the path we ourselves did pave,
And surely soon on Mars humanity's intrepid zeal we shall engrave,

Inexorably to the social sciences the scientific method streaked,
Theories, policies, interventions—cause and effect, rightly, must be critiqued,
And of course their empirical veracity must be concrete else they must be tweaked,

But from a good thing,
Often too much we're tempted to wring,

From music and art,
Friendship and affairs of the heart,
We best keep icy logic apart,
Tis not that to these an illogic we should try to impart,
But that from their immanent dream logic we should never depart,

For the sublime can only be experienced in surreal gestalt not in the profane subpart,
Enraptured—into their Daliesque reveries heart first we should dart,
Not a dispassionate critic but of the painting an integral part,
Not a clinician over the health of your relationships flipping from chart to chart,
But head-over-heels inebriated with your sweetheart,
Sometimes we humans so wont to ourselves outsmart,
Are better served if instead we downsmart.

Fuck You!

Anathema to modern man that at the mercy of the universe he stands,
That so much of both good and bad are out of his hands,
That all his will and his best-laid plans,
Only his odds—at most—expands,

Adamantly does he deny,
As defeatist superstition does he decry,
The truth that of all the forces between this earth and the sky,
That his is but one causal try,
Hence that all his endeavors for their success must rely,
On all the other forces in unison being his trusty ally,

Dare not you question the dogma of 'You reap ONLY what you sow',
At the very least you're a whinger wallowing in your woe,
At worst—a subversive socialist foe,
How convenient for those who than you have 'earned' way, way more dough!

But of course there's no conspiracy—no, no,
There needn't be one for not from above but from below,
Neath the modern capitalist sun doth most favorably grow,
Those good little seedlings who when fighting from the soil to first show,
Dogmatically 'know',
That every iota of effort garners a commensurate reward—a fair quid pro quo,
Therefore, a lack thereof and you're dead as a dodo,

Now what of effort's sum and rate,
If each did critically evaluate,
And got the simple truth straight:
That try as hard as you may—you can't negate,
That your outcomes are subject to vagaries which collectively we may call fate?
Surely, then, effort will abate,
Leaving man's micro and macro dreams less likely to eventuate,

So of course society would have you an eager-beaver schmuck,
The moderner with blind pluck,
To whom as dirty a word as fuck,
Has become the word luck!

Routine Cuck

Routine is to modernity,
What ritual was to antiquity,
Figures since both rely on the same neural instrumentality,

Take the most tedious trudge,
If the ball to get rolling you can somehow budge,
Your brain then via dopamine continually gives it a nudge,
Breadcrumbing you to the mountaintop—the prize for your drudge,

Back then rolling the rock up the hill,
Was for the ancients in-and-of-itself enough to fulfill,
For doing so appeased and pleased the gods' then God's will,
And the cherry on top: unquestionably blessings would flow downhill,
If not in this world then surely in the next so have faith and wait until,

But nowadays it's all the more tough,
For the ancients' magical thinking—we've called its bluff,
No proof of the pudding here-and-now—and we summarily rebuff,
So 'All for naught!' modern man is oft left lamenting after her huff-and-puff,

Yet, dutiful dopamine with its persistent pluck,
As ever sweetens the chase for empty ends that turn out to suck,
I'm like an atheist who can't the habit of daily prayer buck,

I make my bed, do a good job, fix dinner, listen to the missus, do the dishes,
Then rinse-and-repeat until the grim reaper kisses,
I cannot not for something towards task completion pushes,
Yet, at the end of the day, none of these makes true my wishes,

On a neurotransmitter treadmill inclined to get stuck,
Can't jump off—a lame duck,
For worldly transcendence—not without incredible opportunity and luck,
Modern man a routine cuck.

Lost & Find

Flipping through its dusty yellowing leaves searching for this word,
I came across another—more interesting—then another... then a third,
My original aim spurned—my curiosity was spurred,

Reminiscing those halcyon Saturday mornings once my cartoons were done,
I had no choice but to watch cooking and the news—not nearly as fun,
But I'm glad I couldn't shun,
For that which I would've never chosen: that rando docu or old re-run,
Unveiled varying viewpoints—showed me how worlds not my own spun,

Once in a park for hours I got lost,
Scared then but grateful now for my wayward walkabout what wonder crisscrossed,

Now I'm sure to find exactly the content I seek,
No serendipitous rabbit holes that pique,
Google and YouTube seem to know before I even type or speak,
Me in my bubble they keep; no ventilation, stuffy—of me it doth reek,
It's a Matrix kind of bleak,

Luring us to look only in the mirror,
Internet, you promised to invite all the different to dinner, how did you so error?

Indeed tis by letting in all that's not me—that's other,
I bloom bigger and better, else me myself I smother,

Whoever said '*It's the journey not the destination*',
Only had half the explanation,
For it's as much about the wide-eyed, child-like detours, the drifting deviation,
Just ask Columbus about the glories of bad navigation,

So if you veer 'off course'—not deserted island think treasure trove of humankind,
The only compass you need to bring is an open mind,
You're lucky: they let you get lost—find!

Pro-Crastinator

Procrastination a deadly modern sin:
'Thou shalt not wait to thy task begin',

Now, doing the laundry and taking out the trash bin,
Undergoing a prostate exam or a mammogram annually at the min,
And all their scary or unpleasant or drudge kin,
Where a lot or all could be lost if a stitch in time is not sewed in,
Putting them off—obviously no gain therein,
Nevertheless procrastination hath benefits twin,

If your opus be served best,
By a creative spark's zest,
Or when by inspiration possessed,
If to a masterpiece you wish to see it progressed,
Your work's better off, I suggest,
When you ignore productivity's berating behest,

Even modernity that drill-sergeant brainwashed by the logic of the market,
Must concede that oft achieving or bettering an output target,
Than by monomaniacally working your darndest,
Is realized far more efficiently when a magical eureka moment is harnessed,

And, if waiting for the light bulb moment isn't why,
There's still a reason to your marching orders defy,

Yes, some tasks we so dread,
That we'd do anything else instead,
But when we weigh the pros and cons in our head,
Do them we must—to this conclusion we are necessarily led,

But if by cultural compulsion,
Our thoughtful pauses are guilted into expulsion,
From task to task ever in a state of propulsion,
The worthwhile from the pointless—how can we hope to make that avulsion?

Also, each one of us as busy as a bee,
Surely, this benefits the owners-that-be—so conspiracy?
No, no—here there's nothing to see,
Just another well-meaning prompting—we all can agree,
Best taken with a pinch of salt is all I plea,
For along with its cons, some pros for thee and we,
Case in point: I've been meaning to finish this book for a decade now—gee!
A proud pro-crastinator you could definitely call me.

Furlough O'clock

Tick-tock...
I'm on the clock,
Even when my work cell the jailer doth unlock,

Phew! I clock-out,
But, alas, I've only turned the hourglass 180 about,
Weekends—same, same—just twice about then cue the Sunday night pout,

Sure, I admonish myself—don't peep,
Yet in the short-lived peace, I hear for me the sand weep,
As clock-in ominously slithering ever closer doth creep,

And don't you dare call my time 'spare',
As if without your 'work'—I don't exist—I'm not there,

I'm better than drudgery yo!
With passions and projects I'm aglow,
But oft before their magic beans I can even sow,
And even when I'm all set to grow,
Long before I get into a state of flow,
The black hole of time sold becomes my mortal foe,
Who to the self-portraiture of my soul deals a stillbirth deathblow,

Besides, after work ain't my 'own time'—oh no,
For half the time, I spend it merely recovering ever so slow,

From the workday and workweek that I had to undergo,
Then I have to ready myself to give it all another heave-ho,

The fine line between labor and living though,
Many a life-coach for profit purports to show,
Here's what from the tightrope walk of work-life balancing first-hand I know:
From the grind I am only ever granted but a furlough.

Modern Urn

Man's search for meaning, needless to say, far predates modernity,
But unlike that of blissfully ignorant antiquity,
Ours is a disquietingly enlightened odyssey,
All too often shipwrecked in the frigid uncompromising waters of reducibility,

For you see, no pursuit from heaven to the circus,
Through your magnum opus,
If you infinitely regress beneath its surface,
In the biggest picture has any cosmic purpose,

But when you can, you often tend to, and when you do—at that very moment,
When you begin to reduce your meaning: unpack each constituent component,
You set yourself up to soon come eyeball-to-eyeball with its greatest opponent,

For therein you will be horrified,
To find that from the whole the primordial pieces you have pried,
Never again into meaningfulness can be unified,
Meaning—alas, you have Humpty-Dumptyfied,

And why you ask meaningfulness you cannot recompose?
Because the deeper and deeper you decompose,
The more you realize that the meaningful the universe doth 'compose',
Is of the very same inanimate building blocks from which the meaningless arose,
And randomly or for ends its own—not for the ones you grandiloquently suppose,
Thereby giving them an eerie equivalence which nihilistically meaning doth depose,

What a devil's bargain modernity herein doth propose!
What a tightrope dilemma doth it pose!
For modernity, of course, its largesse bestows,
By taking every phenomenon we know, searching for its embryos,
Then casting those too into reductionism's throes,

And so, each of us in turn,
Oh, how well we learn,
To habitually spurn,
The once sacred and whole—to watch it burn,
Only to be condemned to a limbo of no return,
When we are forced to intern,
Our meanings' ashes in an oh so modern urn.

Prisoner's Dilemma

They say 'Absence makes the heart grow fonder',
But of the heart kept apart there is much more to ponder,

We uncritically assume that distance for the soul,
Works like food for the hungry—but that's not the story whole,

Via analogy let's empathize,
As—frying pan to the fire—a prisoner in such a predicament might agonize,

Sure, at first when incarcerated,
Their freedom castrated,
An inmate will long for their old life—this much is undebated,
But here their journey meets a fundamental fork in the road—it's bifurcated,

'You never know what you have until you lose it'—most will lament and eulogize,
Their former lives they will romanticize,
But some who started with such rose-tinted eyes,
Out of depressive-realism or delusion or plain old bitterness sour till they despise,
In hindsight they cringe with disenchanted hind-sighs,

Cocooned in cellular rumination,
Taken for granted holy cows dissected with each iteration of investigation,
Hitherto invisible cracks pried with evermore castigation,
This all tumultuously terminating with their previous value-system's decapitation,

Then our inmate in a wretched double-bind embedded:
Prison abject but release dreaded,
And if freedom granted with society on a collision course headed,

Now this metaphor in modern life impactful all the more,
For never to any age before,
Has mainstream ostracism been so core,

But it's not the 'push' to marginalize that is mostly to blame,
I'd argue that it's much less than the past or at the very most the same,
Far more so it's that modern culture over-sensitizes: thins our skin leaving us lame,
Now every sleight a stick or stone—nothing can be both bad but also tame,
And then the moment you feel even a tad left out or a bit of shame,
There are whole disaffected communities who on your misery lay claim,
Well-organized and vehement, they compellingly frame,
That you're the victim of gross systemic injustice—so society is fair game,

The loner that never knew Pa,
The incel living with but hating Ma,
The Muslim youth that doesn't feel quite right joining friends at the bar,
Acne and braces—the dork with the interests bizarre,
The school shooter, the terrorist, the white supremacist—in the making they are,
The fragile's door modernity has left dangerously ajar,
First it makes you a cry baby then throws you to the 'wolves' to spar,
So victim to victimizer—in the throes of the prisoner's dilemma—a leap not too far.

Goodness Forsake

Being 'good' in any age,
Was and is all about submitting to your desires encage,
To avoid propriety and piety's blame,
Self-denial always the name of the game,

And to this all-wrapped-up-in-a-neat package feel-good exchange if you acquiesced,
Resolutely resisting those tantalizing temptations—the devil's behest,
The more your instincts from the carnal to the material you suppressed,
The more you were supposed to be blessed,

Now here is where modernity away from the past doth crucially cleave,
Then it was be 'good' and believe,
And the rest to god or karma leave,
For being 'good' only in the hereafter will you your rewards receive,
This way the living could never really be aggrieved,
For their just desserts: be it eternal life, 72 virgins or to of suffering be relieved,
Whatever their faiths may have concocted and conceived,
Could never conclusively remain unachieved,

But now for being 'good',
What you deserve—in this here life—get you should, you should!

But of course the world unlike 'god's grace',
Is hardly a fair place,

And unlike when we orgy in sin and morality shirk,
Self-abnegation is often excruciating work,
So the harsh reality that the world's oft a jerk,
Is more than a cause merely of modern irk,

Indeed, having no recourse but on the 'Just World Fallacy' to rely,
Is one among many causes, though few identify,
Of depression that very modern epidemic which none can deny,
Though our tearing mind's eyes we fight back with forced smiles—our battle cry,
In its black sludgy tomb too many of us moderners mummify,

When I try and I try,
But my lot goes awry,
And sometimes my fate my efforts even seem only to damnify,
To the modern river of tears this tributary doth yet more woe supply,
So goodness forsake—to this let's not turn a blind eye.

Glass Revealing

Through this here glass ceiling those peering up and perceiving,
When they butt their heads in achieving,
Are egged on by the culture to keep believing,

But here's what they can't tell you—those preaching:
For so many who are moralized and cajoled to keep reaching,
They don't merely land—THUD!—from so leaping,
They crash right through their flimsy floors below of tissue paper weaving,
Their self-worth weeping,
Meaninglessness creeping,

And here's what's intriguing:
All those cut-throat competing,
Can't seem to figure out for themselves how it's all so self-defeating,
That there's more than just Northward dreaming,
That, in fact, there's Eastward to Westward seeking,
And, off the beaten path—even when you go careening,
Far from ending up reeling,
You'll, for sure, find on your adventures something redeeming,
For it's when coloring outside the lines that the rainbows are truly beaming,

Why you ask is everyone these days such a depressed and anxious goody two shoes,
Who to open their ears and eyes '*lah-lah-lah...*' so adamantly refuse,
Who'd rather than take the elixir called living all their marbles lose?

Well, it's late-stage capitalism's gargantuan promises slathered on so thick,
Seductive with a silver-tongue so slick,
Along with the sneaky trick,
Of commodifying and co-opting any hint of lateral non-conformity so quick,
And selling it back to you though insipid and impotent yet with the silly shtick,
That such banal consumption with a mere tap or click,
Somehow makes you anything you want to be from bad-ass to Bolshevik,
Whereas all you've done is pad profits and capitalism bootlick,

Tis indeed ironic and revealing,
That in this age, supposedly, of individualistic preening,
Far from trying every which way—on the winds of fancies free-wheeling,
That narcissistic lemmings, panting and heaving,
Looking only skyward in single-file off the cliff keep proceeding,
When—a hair's breadth abreast to their right and left—life is teeming.

Quaranreeling

I lay on satin sheets and peer through golden bars,
At the seasons painting Renoirs,
And at night, the ivory moon with tinsel stars,

For the first time in a while, maybe ever,
It's the songs of birds that awake me from my desultory dreams nether,

Snug in my climate-controlled suite,
Velvet under my feet,
At my lips every indulgent treat,
At my finger-tips eclectic entertainments entreat,
Appliances, gadgets, concoctions—creature comforts replete,
Luxury which a century ago didn't even kings and queens greet,

But bars, golden irregardless, make a prison cell,
Worse—a perverse kind of hell:
One of those where when we get what we always wanted—meh, well,
This problem pecks: have I been made a fool of all along by over-sell?
The nagging feeling that pining was better than arriving we can't quite quell,
So long lumbering yarns to ourselves we're coaxed to tell,

With this in mind, the lockdown incarceration that billions beset,
To its toxic crux let's get,
It wasn't that we so missed our routine—the very grind that made us fret,
And being isolated from family and friends—this contributor we mustn't forget,
But there's another which is difficult to notice thus easy to neglect,

Though somewhat counter-intuitive, long and indefinite free time—for most—think,
Tantamount to solitary confinement—it drives them to the psychological brink,

And no amount of comfort nor company can remedy,
In its entirety the symptomology of this malady,

Only the genuinely creative—a miniscule minority,
Can flower fully freed of monotony,

The rest are liable to be afflicted be it by malevolent ideology,
Personal psychopathology,
Interpersonal animosity,
Or at the very least by draining dramaturgy,

The reason? For pure abstraction most have no proclivity hence no affinity,
Therefore upon to 'think' they need real and present 'tangible' objects positively,
'*Small minds discuss people, average minds discuss events...*'—most definitely,
And in regards to these objects that self-same lack of abstract acuity,
Comes back to haunt in the form of non-sequitur and absurdity,
In this case put on steroids by time to 'think' unto infinity,
And crucially which given that we are dealing with objects of reality,
If acted upon can reach the extreme of committing atrocity,

The idle mind truly is the Devil's workshop—no homily inanity,
An unenviable dilemma I foresee for most of humanity:
Toil in drudgery or teeter toward insanity,

The Pandemic was a natural experiment like no other—a real mind crusher,
So let's be ready if robotics and AI the Jetsons Age usher,
We'd better rocket launch our creativity and intellect up and upper,

Just cut me loose from the relentless rat-race—I thought I'd flourish freewheeling,
But it was quite revealing quarantining,
In the prison of my own mind I was left deranged staring at the ceiling,
Preyed upon by the devilish, disturbing and dangerous—I was sent quaranreeling.

Bitterer Lemonache

When life gives you lemons make lemonade,
The cards you're dealt deftly played,
In any age, circumstance or place is the best of all moves that can be made,
A case where if you're by common sense swayed,
Thereby rationality will be honored not betrayed,

One logical inference herein implied,
Is that if with the bitterest lemons, the worst cards you're supplied,
Then if this fact the sweetness of your lemonade does not solely decide,
At the very least with its sweetness will countervailingly collide,

There's seemingly no heresy here,
Irregardless of however austere,
It does as nothing but reason sheer appear,
Which is true—that is until modern expectations adhere,

With what you've been given be the best you can be,
Is hardly an undergirding implicit nor overarching explicit modern decree,

In fact, polar opposite to the contrary,
Bombarding with the rare rags-to-riches biography—revisionist very,
We are influenced to never be satisfied until we achieve the extraordinary,
To never settle until we realize what was formerly only reserved for reverie,

This 'Just do it' because 'Impossible is nothing' mentality,
As with all cultural dogmas, imbued with morality,
Admittedly counter-intuitively, conspires to backfire on rationality,

Here's how it machinates so:
Say one has selected and executed the rational move and although,
Consequently results do flow,
They're underwhelming—for your endeavors you've got nothing much to show,

Now these results all that could be reasonably expected though,
Being beneath your expectations way below,
Disappoint and frustrate you so that this foments an emotional tornado,
Whose irrational gusts of gusto,
Ravage reason leaving your lot likely worse-off if not dealing it a deathblow,
And this can in a vicious cycle downhill go:
Your irrational flailing drives your outcomes low,
And in response an ever more irrational tantrum you throw,
Which in turn your hopes only further torpedo,

So you see being rational in modern life,
Thanks to modern entitlement a tightrope walk—always on the edge of a knife,
The best expectable outcome if mediocre—the cause of much emotional strife,
Making the chances of drowning in bitterer lemonache all the more rife.

Hellfare State

Disadvantaged? Poor?
Dad left? Mom a drunk? Trailer park or hood had to endure?
Disabled? Sick? Old? Future unsure?
Ain't nothing for the can-doer!

Pull yourself up by your own bootstraps,
Watch out! Self-pity insidiously entraps,

Up at dawn's crack, crunches if you want abs,
The Land of Opportunity belongs to he who grabs,
Pound the pavement for scraps,
Want billions? Play share market craps,
Launch rockets, hawk online, design apps,
Upon thought and deed emblazon 'PERSONAL RESPONSIBILITY' in all caps,

Thatcher, Hayek, Reagan and Rand warn of the horror,
Of betraying the man in the mirror,
They consider it the 20th Century's gravest error,

Income, corporate, capital gains—nah—go-getter get that tax evading knack,
'Cause welfare junkies that slack,
Don't deserve jack!

But when most saplings aspire solely to the sun,
When their duty to nurture their own soil they shun,
Hoping that among the few mighty oaks they can be one,

Then safety kills at the point of private handguns,
College only for privilege, legacy admissions, donors' daughters and sons,
Healthcare could leave you homeless or in the slums,
Fast and processed food—disease and early death becomes,

Understandably then the hopeless, sick and dumb—seething at being left behind,
In allergic reaction to their atomized anomie rise up combined,
Lose their collective mind,
Conspiratorial or chemical, in drugs they refuge find,
Then demagogues spellbind,
Them into committing the hitherto unthinkable for they're by now to reason blind,
Hereby, many a vast empire and great nation have unto their demise declined,

So beware those who march single-mindedly to your own drums,
Chanting rugged individualism mantras in tongues,
Railing against the welfare state at the top of your lungs,
Methodically dismantling its rungs,
In the not so long-run,
In the 'Hellfare State'—it's your own self-interest that will come undone.

Protagonist Antagonist

Think your life to an epic novel or film akin,
To be content wherein,
No matter victim, hero or heroine,
Saint or committing sin,
Whether lose or win,
You must be its kingpin,
Leading lady, leading man,
Robin—no can,
You gotta be the Joker or Batman,

To the demise of dad-the-dictator though saying amen,
For men,
Family their fiefdom back when,
'Twas easier back then,

And an omnipotent god up there was installed for all,
Whom, not the other way around, but actually you held in thrall,
Who personally knew and loved you and was available on call,
So that you never ever had to feel small,

While fiction in any age be it happily-ever-after, romantic, dramatic or tragic,
By skillfully employing mirror neurons and the empathetic psychodynamic,
Makes us vicariously the protagonist to work its magic,

Now, our solar systems where I am the sovereign sun tend to be quite robust,
Mischievously modernity, though, into the works has a spanner thrust,
Of lords and ladies then, celebrities and sports stars now—we're not fussed,
They're so far removed from us—ours is but to fantasize and lust,
They might as well be fictional characters as above discussed,
No—tis only our peers, those just like us, who can leave us in their dust,
Who have the power to our 'BIG FISH in a small pond' bubbles bust,
For man a social animal so this power over us necessarily have they must,
This is just an analogy so snowflakes don't self-combust:
Like into the segregated White peace Black kids bussed,
Into our small ponds too many peer fish social media has brusquely gushed,

Marauders each,
Who nowadays easily my psychic palace's moats breach,
Their omnipresent narratives my own dilute and pollute—its preeminence leech,
As to usurp my protagonist throne these antagonists reach.

UnSocratic Method

'*The unexamined life is not worth living*',
But humbly, oh great Socrates, regarding reflection I've got a misgiving,

What makes all the difference when I reflect,
Is how I vivisect,

Be it the social, political or economic at which my thoughts I direct,
Or when upon the personal I introspect,
If not through a dispassionate-learned-rational-philosophical lens I dissect,
But glancing through its antithesis—the laymen's lens—I inspect,
The consequences are wont to be abject,

In terms of the super-structure this is quite obvious I suspect,
Mustachioed to orange when the masses the wrong man did elect,
The rest was almost the end of history—the last I checked,
And the same again I fully expect,

The fallacies that flow,
From amateur introspection are less plain to see though,
Nevertheless, they too, down-the-line, can devastate or deliver the deathblow,

Yet, despite all the disaster in store—of which only we well know,
And hence are duty bound to break down blow-by-blow,
We kowtow—for tis a big modern NO-NO,
For the expert or professional thinker to disabuse Jill & Joe Schmo,

So around their epistemologies evasively we must tip-toe,
Their opinions and thoughts are sovereign—the ultimate zone of NO-GO,
Trespassers will be shot! Questions shall not follow!

Come hell to me or high-water to the world although,
Critical stones thou shalt not throw,
Worship 'I' the false idol—the modern ego,
On the unsocratic method's pew kneeling low.

Oxyfatalism

Every man's psyche within,
Blowin' in the neural wind a subliminal solipsistic echo makes it seem herein:
That every big decision and action I partake in,
Matters to the great-scheme-of-things' columns of loss and win,
Understandable since subjectively around each 'I' a world does spin,
And of course this echo modernity has loudened to an unendurable din,

If the weight of the world has become too much for you to bear and grin,
With this big bang begin:
Save to the worlds of your closest kith and kin,
Nothing you do means a thing—to think and act otherwise is your original sin,

For there's only two kinds of people:
The world changers and the sheeple,

Now before you accuse me of being nihilistic,
Be assured that this is no such polemic—indeed it's quite optimistic,

Hitler, Trump, Gandhi, King,
Evil, obnoxious, sagacious, courageous—let them be anything,
It matters not—what only counts are the momentous changes they could ring,
But what historic consequence from my petty decisions and actions spring?

So if I don't affect millions,
Since I'm neither president, revolutionary nor is my net worth in the billions,

Why, then, as if I matter to the big pic,
And given that feeding my family in the First World is fairly basic,
Do I worry myself sick?

And worse, despite how much I agonize over each decision and action I take,
Only a house of cards I can ever hope to make,
For when the powers-that-be and the system quake,
In rubble my dreams are left in its wake,

The faithful were unburdened by accepting that each plays but a bit part,
And that the best-laid plans fate can laughingly tear apart,
And since this is true of the temporal too—modern man so smart,
Really should take this lesson to heart,

And, to the 'sheeple' epithet if you vehemently push back,
Yes, maybe you're not the blind follower type who critical faculties lack,
But that still leaves you, like me, with the rest of the pack:
Who's got no choice but to toe-the-line in fear of facing furious flak,
Yet whose reward for being a good soldier is oft only capricious blowback,

It may appear like oxymoronism,
To proclaim powerlessness a much-needed escapism,
But tis a vaccine to the modern superbug of solipsism,
So, que será, será, take the truth serum—take a shot of oxyfatalism.

Stretch Marx

Modern man from society, the economy and the polity,
Demands all life's goods—in all their variegated variety,
With an infallibility of reliability:
Economic growth with equality,
Productivity with humanity,
Indulgence with sustainability,
Technology with anthropocentricity,
Rule of law with liberty,
Justice with pity,
The greater good with inalienability,
Progressiveness with traditionality,
Disagreement with civility,
Commonality with diversity,
Belongingness with individuality,
Status with egality,
Self-actualization with financial security,
Trade-offs? NO! We will entertain none such in spite of reality!

So here's an antidote to expectations grown so grand,
That they make modern man oft crash land,

The economy, society and the polity exist structurally,
For the proletariat by the bourgeoisie,
The working by the owning to be exploited—exclusively,

Now just because Marx diagnosed the problem accurately,
Doesn't mean that his solution, unfortunately,
Isn't far worse than the problem by some degree, at least up until presently,

For capitalism undeniably,
Better than any system tried alternatively,
Doth incomparably burgeon our wealth materially,

Yet, what we can take from Marx, consolingly,
Is that since the economy, society and the polity as constituted currently,
Are good for one thing and one thing only:
Satisfying the bottom of Maslow's Hierarchy,
Food, shelter, safety—survival—solely,
It is within not without we must look to if we are to live wholly,
So extrapolate from your soul's throbbing heart eccentrically,
On your Marx—stretch your imaginations expansively.

Whose Dreams?

That adults as far as possible in some shape or form,
Recreate their childhood—it's no great insight that this is the norm,

To the heartbreaking extent,
That abuse victims whom in torturous suffering their childhoods have spent,
Grow up to on loved ones oft inflict the same wretched torment,

Though this inter-generational transmission is commonplace,
With a significant implication of it we've obliviously not come face-to-face,

Ask yourself how many kids prefer school and homework to video games and TV?
Veggies to ice-cream and candy?
Cleaning their rooms to mucking about in a pigsty carefree?
Early bedtime or frolicking till hours wee?
The answer's obvious—you can't honestly disagree,

Setting the undeniable virtues of delayed gratification aside,
There's an indoctrination implied:
That which you desire by the very fact you desire it only serves to misguide,
Therefore, save as a guilty pleasure, must be self-denied,

But this in turn is antithetical in the extreme,
To the very modern theme,
Expressed by the dictums 'Do what you love' and 'Follow your dream',

Unless, of course, what you have 'dreamed',
Is amongst those which into your mind have been streamed,
Only because by the status quo worthy they have been deemed,

So parental advisory: that down to the minute scripted childhood,
School, homework, extra tutoring, recitals—all well-meaning and good,
To another of your claimed aims run afoul could,

If 'As long as it makes them happy' be your final destination,
Know that you are raising adults who can't resist the urge of self-abnegation,
Whereas, if they were capable of pursuing their authentic aspiration,
They could be more fulfilled in the ultimate calculation,
And this is so even if their dreams do not necessarily culminate in consummation,

Through books and movies of true stories I safely peep,
At the brave who've loved and lived by plunging headlong into the deep,
'*One day, one day, soon!*' I promise myself as to the tried-and-tested I keep,

Into my dream can I awaken from the sleep?
Will I ever be able to take the leap?
Or am I too good a sheep?

Creative Destruction

Save my limbs and my thinking wings,
But sometimes, just sometimes I wish to lose all my life's 'good' things,
I know the self-destructive death-wish tone this rings,

But I can't help myself from resenting them so,
And it's precisely and perversely because they're way too good to let go,

See, I've been taught to love them: they're all I have to show,
They're my life's work and worth, my clinical pinnacle—I know, I know,
But that also spells—'The End'—there's nothing more, well except though,
The abyss below,

Thence I'm stuck in rational Groundhog Day,
Most things, most of the time, kinda sorta at least, going my way,
Hence nothing really against which to inveigh,
So smiling whilst underneath white-knuckling to keep banality at bay,
Convincing myself to stay,
'*There's nothing beyond the horizon*'—rationalizing intrusive dreams away,
I'm bathed in warm sunshine but guiltily finding it cold and gray,

I'm tempted, I am, to go the nuclear option—BOOM!
Like movie heroes whom,
Stride away tall unscathed against destruction's impending doom,

But 'sanity' returns all too soon,
To keep me safe and sound of mind in my cocoon,

Statistically, far more likely than fairytale endings are the converse,
Definitely off-the-beaten-path if I traverse,
It's gonna hit hard on the purse,
I could end up destitute or worse,
Besides, all progress is change but not the reverse,

Tis true '*The mass of men lead lives of quiet desperation...*' as Thoreau trolled,
But my shoulders are not so strong and bold,
The burden of hara-kiri not even in theory can they hold,

Go on— 'cause at myself I too now and then snigger,
But pulling the trigger,
Would need a man than me bigger,

This is masochistically why,
Though if you ask me I will flat-out deny,
I find myself secretly wishing that out of nowhere, by the by,
A metaphorical meteor would crash into my life blowing it sky-high,
Letting me free to spread my wings and fly,
To what and wheresoever roves my mind's eye,
But crucially not making me the bad guy.

Roid Rage

Anything that is good or desirable deemed,
Is seized by the profit motive with technology teamed,
Put on 'steroids' it seems then to the whole world streamed and screamed,

On 'steroids' working longer,
On 'steroids' athletes stronger,
On 'steroids' movies slicker,
On 'steroids' lips thicker,
On 'steroids' communicating quicker,
On 'steroids' Tinder only reason you pick her,
On 'steroids' convenience faster,
On 'steroids' climate disaster,
On 'steroids' smiles so much bigger,
That depression on 'steroids' doth it trigger,

But tis more than to mental health and the planet the obvious harm,
Tis an affront to the transcendence that is charm,
See aesthetics owes much to the natural only just accentuated,
Tis 'Reality Plus' consecrated,
Not inflated nor deflated unto the point that it is desecrated,
Take a beautiful woman's face,
The baby jawline and demure chin—its cherubic grace,
If I were to retrace,
With unreally miniscule proportions—I would caricature thereby debase,
In the other direction, take the body builder meat-head,

In this case real steroids used to gain and shred,
His impossibly muscled mass of all fat shed,
Attractive? Or gross instead?

If only on 'steroids' were but a few,
True—via contrast I'd be amused by the view,
But seemingly when all,
Are in the 'steroids' thrall,
Its adulterations evermore gaudy and gargantuan with ginormous gall,
I feel alienated as this hyper-reality sprawls,
I get this 'roid rage' at the carnage—my aesthetic sensibility it appalls.

I Quit

Winners never quit; quitters never win,
WARNING: Infectious! The quitter a modern leper plus sin,
Countless books and courses preaching grit—parents, it's never too early to begin,
Posts, quotes and posters egg on reminding us to go 110% all-in to the fin,
But the more fanatical the zeal to never ever give in,
The more likely that any hope of clarity therein,
As to what exactly we're clawing tooth-and-nail for will be lost in the spin,

Most of your tasks at work uselessly Sisyphean,
But you keep plugging away being a good peon?

The years prove that your significant other will never change for the better,
But in marriage counseling you wash your dirty linen with a therapist abettor?

Not a struggling artist starving pursuing your passion,
A foot-soldier fighting someone else's battle forced to show no compassion?

Your hard-earned dollar you know it's wise to ration,
But to keep up appearances freehanded you follow fad and fashion?

Is this to which I'm giving of myself every last little bit,
Minus all the religious and cultural bullshit,
And the profiteering propaganda from the puppeteers' pulpit,
Really in my and/or society's best interests legit?

And even if giving-up your individual bottom-line will at first hard-hit,
Given others are likely to the cause commit,
Granted, usually a very big 'if' I admit,
Is it so that if enough fellow serfs too do it,
Everyone will benefit?
Then quit!

Civiliezational Kool-Aid

She peered cooped within your Mercedes Benz,
At me the disheveled philosopher—but then she soon had to cleanse,
Her eyes off the man who dangerous drivel pens,

As many a night we lay,
In a cold creaky matchbox studio whose rent I couldn't pay,
I recited her a lullaby hoping she would stay,
But knowing its very own 'happy' ending meant there was no way,

'No rules, no norms, no chains of society',
'No work, no chores, no monotony',
'We could love who we want, we weren't sold into the bonds of matrimony',
That's when piqued she turned but uncomfortably,
'You and I and everyone else were once free—absolutely!',
'*Garden of Eden?*', she interjected. 'Not exactly',
'Since we could steal and rape and murder wantonly',
'Life was '*...solitary, poor, nasty, brutish and short*' abjectly',
'*Ok...*', she prompted me to go on interestedly,

'So we left behind the evolutionary forest'. '*Reluctantly?*',
'Arguably, quite possibly',
'We built all this systematically',
'Now life is social, rich, kind, cultured and long—relatively',
'*We sacrificed our freedom for stuff and safety, basically?*',
'Precisely',

'*So it wasn't the Garden of Eden but hell, really*',
'*And, it wasn't some forbidden fruit delicacy*',
'*We didn't risk it all for some indulgent pleasure foolishly*',
'*We did the smart thing, actually?*',
She, herself, recoiled, ambivalently,
Then she began to get dressed to leave, as usual hurriedly,

'But here's the thing sweetheart...',
I entreated her not to depart,

'What if a starving artist who has to sell his precious paint...', she sat,
'To buy canvas and food, sells too much such that...',
'*He has a big canvas...*' , her reasoning fighting itself to stand pat,
'*But not enough paint? It's late*', she hastened out of the flat,

A clarinet wind whistled menthol rain suffused with flickering neon indigo,
Through the cracks of the cello-taped window,
Onto the hard mattress on the moldy wooden floor below,

'*A painter mustn't sell too much paint, right?*',
'If it only were so easy...', she sat up, her eyes reflected the lava lamp twilight,
'Canvas is a wholesale business—you swallow the apple whole outright',
'*What do you mean?*'. 'Wouldn't do much good to give the green light...',
'To pick and choose which freedoms to give up, which rules to obey. It might...',
'*Leave us back at square one*'. 'Exactly! The '*...nasty, brutish and short*' blight',

'Civilization is far more of a sure bet...'. '*If we drink the 'Kool-Aid'!*',
'Ha, yeah! Lock, stock and peril—down to every insanity, inanity, lie and charade',

'But you know what? For most, I'd say, it's a good trade',
At my evenhandedness she seemed disappointed and dismayed,
'Most aren't going to be good painters, I'm afraid',
'*So why not sell all their 'paint' for stuff and security??*', she retorted betrayed,

'It is only the true artist, the man with soul...', down my course I stayed,
'*To whom the 'Kool-Aid' is poisoned with cyanide*', she completed looking frayed,

Breaking script, she didn't hurriedly dress nor look at her watch with fret,
Against the macaroon moon she cut a pensive silhouette,

Until, at her lychee lips an amber ocean brooding to the brim,
She snipered the jazz whispered contemplation, '*Shall I leave him?*',

'*Am I a true artist?*',
'Or better off as a cookie-cutter conformist?',

'You've been coming here for years',
'*And each night running back from my fears!*',

'Even the true artist has to eat—just not too much', this echoed on repeat,
He swooped into kiss her forehead, a profound bass heartbeat,
Her epiphany was such that all the lies and deceit,
Which metastasized into the guilt with which her psyche she had browbeat,
Wafted away into the dank bohemian street,
For her it was neither right to run away with him in passion's heat,
Nor stay faithful to the patriarchal beast submitting in soul crushing defeat,
No, 'twas only the equilibrium of the 'illicit' affair so dialectically sweet,
Which could make her alive and complete.

www.ingramcontent.com/pod-product-compliance
Lightning Source LLC
LaVergne TN
LVHW081317110826
845149LV00006B/1529

* 9 7 8 0 9 9 2 5 8 3 7 6 7 *